In a Village Far from Home

In a Village Far From Home

My Life among the Cora Indians of the Sierra Madre

Catherine Palmer Finerty

THE UNIVERSITY OF ARIZONA PRESS TUCSON

The University of Arizona Press
© 2000 The Arizona Board of Regents
All Rights Reserved

☉ This book is printed on acid–free, archival–quality paper
Manufactured in the United States of America
First printing

Library of Congress Cataloging–in–Publication Data
Finerty, Catherine Palmer, 1908–
In a village far from home : my life among the Cora Indians of the Sierra
Madre / Catherine Palmer Finerty.
    p. cm.
ISBN 0–8165–2037–2 (pbk. : alk. paper)
1. Cora Indians–Social life and customs. 2. Cora Indians–Religion. 3. Cora
Indians–Medicine. 4. Ethnobotany–Mexico–Jesús María (Nayar)
5. Traditional medicine–Mexico–Jesús María (Nayar) 6. Jesús María (Nayar,
Mexico)–Social life and customs. I. Title.
F1221.C6 F56 2000
306′.0972′42–dc21   99–050961

British Cataloguing–in–Publication Data
A catalogue record for this book is available from the British Library.

Publication of this book is made possible in part by the proceeds of a
permanent endowment created with the assistance of a Challenge Grant
from the National Endowment for the Humanities, a federal agency.

For Barbara, who taught me
to give shots in an orange
and who told me to write this book,
and for Polly, who kept me going
when the going was rough

Contents

Introduction

*T*his is an almost true account of how a naive American woman
became involved with Cora Indians and mountain Mexicans
in a small town in a bottom pocket of the Sierra Madre Occidental.

It is not a story. It has no plot, no sex, no violence, not even a
moral. It is simply a succession of personal adventures, some funny,
some scary, a few tragic, as the American woman found herself more
and more involved in the life of a town so remote that it was not on
her map of Mexico.

I was the woman, and the town was Jesús María.

Jesús María was probably the most unprepossessing little town
in western Mexico. It was thirty minutes from Tepic by air, eight days
by mule. When I first flew into it, there were no roads leading into it
from anywhere, possibly because no town had any business being
there at all.

It was in a totally inhospitable location. Stretched out on a ledge
above a tropical river and hemmed in on all sides by mountains, it
was so hot it was known as the oven of the Sierra. In the dry season, a
scorching wind blew up from the south with a stinging cargo of sand,
grit, gravel, and manure. In the rainy season, the clouds rolled down
from the north and drenched the town. When the sun came out, the
very earth steamed. The only times the heat abated were on some
winter nights and during the annual unexpected winter rain, and
then it turned clammily cold.

There were other discomforts. The town was as hospitable to insects as it was hostile to humans. It harbored more than its fair share
of scorpions and so many small biting insects that almost everyone
itched somewhere almost all of the time.

It was a town without a single one of the luxuries I had always
taken for granted: running water, bathtubs, telephones, newspapers,

sidewalks, ice. The blistering sun burned my skin. The rock–paved roads bruised my feet. There were no Americans to complain to, no television to criticize, and the two news programs from Texas came through on my transistor radio only late at night.

Clearly, a town so ill favored had to have some powerful attraction or I would have flown out the next time the little plane flew back in. What snared me was that, in between planes, I discovered that in and around Jesús María I could be of use, an irresistible inducement to just about any woman past retirement age.

For eight long, fascinating years, aided and abetted by doctors both in Mexico and the United States and by the Franciscans, who forgave me for being a Protestant, I practiced medicine with no credentials whatever, volunteering my services and, with the help of friends, providing the medicine free. It was a new life I could never have foreseen and one for which I shall always bless my quite undeserved good fortune.

As time went on, both Indians and Mexicans introduced me to their rituals and invited me into their lives. That is what this book is about.

The real name of the town is Jesús María, but I have changed the names of my friends who live there to preserve their privacy.

In writing this, I have juggled the dates a little but not much. Some of the conversations are verbatim, written down immediately. Some are as I remember them. A very few are invented. (If the people didn't always say exactly what I say they did, they ought to have.)

Except for a few of the Indians who speak only their own tongue, the people in Jesús María speak colloquial Spanish. I have not translated what they say literally but into colloquial English. They are not quaint, and I do not want them to appear so. It is the least I can do to repay the many bounties I have received at their kind and generous hands.

In a Village Far from Home

1

What Is That Woman Doing Here?

The bishop was waiting for his mail at the top of the hill. I came struggling up it behind the burro that was carrying my bags. I introduced myself.

"I had the honor of photographing you at the mission of Santa Clara," I reminded him as I handed him the letters the pilot had given me. "Do you remember me, Señor?"

The bishop looked at me attentively for a moment. Then, "No," he said kindly.

The bishop's own house, the *curato*, was the only place for me to stay in Jesús María. There were no inns or guest houses. The little mission plane that had flown me out from Tepic had pirouetted on the sandy airstrip and buzzed off up the canyon, not to return for seven days.

I was stuck.

Moreover, I had the very strong impression that, exquisitely courteous as he was, the bishop was not pleased to receive me. I could only wonder what on earth had impelled me to thrust myself, uninvited, into this uninviting slot in the mountains of western Mexico.

Nobody needed me here. I had nothing to give or even to sell. I was not here to study or buy. I was simply on a self-appointed tour of the Franciscan missions buried amid the peaks and gorges of the Sierra Madre Occidental, and Jesús María didn't even have a mission. It was simply the seat of the Franciscan missionary bishopric. For some unfathomable reason, I had thought to pay my respects to the bishop. He didn't even remember me.

With the burro pattering along ahead of us, urged on by kicks from its owner, the bishop and I plodded up the rock–paved street to the church. The stones underfoot were cocoa colored and so sharp they hurt through the soles of my heavy shoes. The little wall–to–wall adobe houses with their bricked–up windows were cocoa colored like the street. The sun blazed down as if it hated us, and I felt sure that I would soon be cocoa colored, too.

There was no one but us in sight except for a runty little spotted pig. It rooted along the side of the road, snorting.

How I happened to be in the Mexican mountains at all was a little puzzling to everyone but me. I had spent more than half of my life in New York City, working in what the innocent regarded as glamour jobs. I had been Helena Rubinstein's advertising manager, vice president of a middle–size advertising agency, beauty editor of a widely circulated fashion magazine. Finally, I was a copy–group head at Batten Barton Durstine and Osborn. New York had been good to me. Everywhere I worked, I had been treated better than I deserved.

My social life was frivolous and pleasant, owing chiefly to the charm and brilliance of my husband. He was a distinguished lawyer who sweetened his practice as special attorney to blue–chip companies with pro bono publico cases for which he would take no fee. He was the only person I had ever known who could quote poetry before breakfast and get away with it.

It was a pleasant life, but, struggling in my office for a new idea or sipping a cocktail in one of the country clubs we belonged to so our children could swim, and sail, and play tennis within the chaperonage of our friends, I often felt a stranger.

Growing up in a quiet little college town in Southern California had not really prepared me either for the hurly–burly of Madison Avenue or the limitations of social life on Long Island. And I came from a long line of pioneers–farmers, most of them–the last of whom had discovered California when it was still new. The West was in my blood.

Eventually, my engaging children, who had somehow survived a working mother, grew up and scattered. My husband, after a long illness, died. I was approaching the time when I could cash in on my agency stock and my profit sharing and be eligible for Social Security.

Many of our friends there on Long Island had died or moved to warmer places. Many of my cohorts at the office were planning their own retirements, in New Hampshire, in Florida, in Greece.

I opted for Mexico.

My husband was much older than I, and I had always sadly known that the day would come when I would be alone, an aging lady of rugged health and restless disposition. I had hoped that when that day came I could retire to California—but the California I had loved as a child was no longer there. It was even hard to remember how it once had been, when one little town with green lawns, and green trees, and flowers had been followed by miles of wilderness, gray with sage and prickly with cacti, and then by another little green town with its trees, and lawns, and flowers. There were orange groves then, but they only introduced a few squares of order in an otherwise beautiful, untamed world. The air was so clear that the mountains, miles away, looked close enough to touch with one's finger.

That was a long time ago. By the time I was ready to leave New York, Southern California had become an endless, murky housing development from the sea to the desert, a land of end-to-end automobiles, of microwaves, and topless bars.

Mexico was like early California, only more so. The towns were smaller. The wildernesses between them were wilder. The sky was vaster. The mountains were more mountainous.

And Mexico offered a challenge. Was it true that nobody could learn a new language after the age of sixty? I began taking Spanish lessons at the New School for Social Research, at night, after a day at the office. Could I perhaps teach English in Mexico? I took courses in that, too, and got myself a night class of Costa Rican girls in a YMCA in Hell's Kitchen, then the section of New York City richest in entries on the police blotter. I made a dash to Guadalajara and bought a house just outside it to make sure I wouldn't lose my nerve.

During the next two years, I got ready to leave. I prepared my husband's papers for the three universities that had asked for them. I gave walls of books to museums, libraries, and law offices. I divided the silver and the better pieces of furniture among my children, and the vanload left over I gave to St. Vincent de Paul. Then I put the house on the market, mailed off the one hundred books the Mexican

government allowed me, packed family papers and the few belongings I thought I couldn't do without into the back of a new VW
squareback, got behind the wheel, and drove myself to Guadalajara
by way of Tucson, Arizona. It was a long road and a lonely one. I had
one friend in Guadalajara. I was sixty-two.

I arrived in Guadalajara exhausted but triumphant and plunged
into the business of living as a foreigner in an alien land. I took Spanish lessons. I read books. I visited museums, went to movies and con-
certs, joined the garden club, made friends and flower arrangements,
and continued to be just as spoiled as any other *gringa* down from
that opulent country over the border to the north who ever set foot
in Mexico.

My friend had secured a maid for me. Instead of having dinner at
two o'clock in the afternoon so my maid could go home and do her
washing, I insisted on dining at night. I gave checks to workers who
couldn't endorse them because they couldn't write their names. I crit-
icized Mexico and Mexicans and was always saying, "Why don't
they . . .?" I was convinced that I couldn't go to sleep at night without
reading in bed, and I needed a cup of coffee before getting up in the
morning. I slept under an electric blanket and was afraid of using a
public bathroom.

Then I got mixed up with the Franciscans.

My next-door neighbor was a lapsed Catholic who invited me to
lunch every Thursday when she made baking-powder biscuits and
fricasseed chicken. There were always other guests there, and on one
occasion I sat next to a young Franciscan priest. He had just taken
over the Huichol Exposition in the Basilica of Zapopan, about a mile
from my house.

The Huichol Exposition was one of my favorite haunts, and I told
the young Franciscan so. He asked me if I would care to work there as
a volunteer.

My life in Guadalajara was a little tame, and I loved the exposition. It was a great temptation to accept his invitation, but I felt that I
was not equipped.

"I speak very little Spanish," I told him.

"We need someone who speaks English," he replied.

"And I'm not a Catholic," I said apologetically.

"That's all right," he said breezily. "You're a nice lady."

I wasn't sure of that, but anyway I headed for the basilica the next morning and started work.

The basilica is a handsome old Franciscan church that probably antedates most of the churches in the west of Mexico. It is both temple and seminary. The actual church is rather small, but it is flanked with long wings on either side and backed up by a high stone square of rooms surrounding a fine old patio behind. The Huichol Exposition was at the end of one of the wings, facing a big atrium within a high wrought–iron fence.

The exposition was nine–tenths museum and one–tenth shop. I worked in the shop. There, a Franciscan friar and I sold the exotic yarn paintings, the hand–woven bags and belts, and the bead jewelry made by the Huichols.

The Huichols were our own Indians. (I had learned early on that Huichol is pronounced "Weechole," with the accent on the second syllable.) They lived in the mountains in the northern part of our own state of Jalisco, so protected by the natural fortress surrounding them that they were said to have preserved their native language, their traditional customs and beliefs, and their integrity as a tribe as no other Indian community in Mexico. Certainly there were no other Indians more decorative personally or more talented artistically than the Huichols. One of the reasons I had loved to go to the exposition was that sometimes I would see Huichols there, gorgeous in their white tunics and loose white trousers, both embroidered with deer, eagles, butterflies, rabbits, peacocks, stars, and geometrics in colored floss. I loved selling the fascinating things that the Huichols made.

The museum part was chiefly an exhibition of photomurals of the Huichols in their own mountain fastness. I timidly wondered if I would ever have the luck to go to the mountains to see them for myself.

The Huichols came to the basilica because the Franciscans took care of them there. The Franciscans gave them a walled–in camping space behind the basilica with a place to wash their clothes. When a Huichol child got sick, it would be a brown–robed Franciscan who talked the suspicious father into letting me take the child to the government hospital. When the health department was immunizing children against polio, TB, measles, and the rest, it was a Franciscan who helped me get the children to the government clinic. When a Huichol child died in the hospital, it was a Franciscan nun who went with me to help me buy a coffin and a young Franciscan priest who walked with the parents behind my squareback as I slowly drove to the cemetery, where he read the burial service.

Having grown up two blocks from the weary road Fray Junípero Serra trudged from California mission to California mission (missions we always proudly showed to our guests from Boston and New York City), being with the Franciscans seemed a little like living in history.

The young priest I had met at my neighbor's house and who was my boss at the exposition had no car. Sometimes I drove him to visit people who needed him. I learned from him to accept the beautiful hospitality of humble homes without being afraid I'd catch something. I learned that it would be hard to overestimate the charm of the Mexican poor in their own houses.

The Franciscans had started mission schools in the Sierra only a few years before. There were several graduates of one of them, supported by the Franciscans, in a house near mine, continuing their education in the government schools in Zapopan. I came to know them well and to love them for their wit, admire them for their talent, and enjoy them for their nice manners.

One of them offered to escort me to the Sierra, to Santa Clara, the mission school they had all attended. With friends from the States assuring me that I was taking my life in my hands, for the Huichols had a fearsome reputation, I accepted the invitation.

It took us a day and a night and half of another day to get to the missions: to Tepic by car, overnight in Tepic, and then in a little plane over a seemingly endless jumble of mountains, to a short gravel strip only recently cut out of the woodlands of oak and pine.

On the flight out, there had been the occasional small cluster of thatched roofs in the most unlikely places below; then nothing but mountains: mountains, mountains, mountains, and no two alike.

The mission was only a few years old. It was the first school the Franciscans had built in the Huichol Sierra after three centuries away. Padre Jacinto, who founded it, had walked through the mountains for a year looking for pupils and had ended up with five, three of them orphans. When my young Huichol friend and I visited it, there were eighty–five students, boys and girls, all boarding, as their homes were miles away across the mountains.

I had never seen a school like the mission of Santa Clara. It bore no resemblance whatever to the beautiful, ruinous old missions in California. It was completely primitive, all of adobe bricks made by hand, with plank doors fastened by thongs wound around spikes thrust into the wood and the wall.

I had never seen such a chapel, made of pines split top to bottom and joined together, bark side outside, with a stone slab for an altar.

I had never seen a group of children so cordial, so decorative, or so happy working at whatever work there was that they could do. They seemed to me all to be handsome, with their lustrous, bronzy skin, their glossy black hair, their dark eyes ever so slightly slanted, their smiling mouths over their almost universally white, even teeth.

I was enchanted with them, as anyone would have to be, and I fell in love with the Franciscan nuns, cheerful mountain Mexican girls who were teachers, nurses, and mothers to all the children in the school. Their sunniness in the absence of any comforts at all made me ashamed of myself. I learned at least one thing from them. I learned that there are four positions in which you can sleep on a bed of wooden boards without bruising a hip. It was an art that stood me in good stead for many years.

When I got back to the Huichol Exposition in the basilica and looked again at the blown–up photographs that covered the walls, I realized better than before how magnificent they were.

Having just come from the Santa Clara mission, however, I couldn't help feeling a lack. The photomurals were almost all purely anthropological. There were almost no pictures of those beguiling children in the schools.

In my innocent enthusiasm, I decided to take some myself. Leaving my work in the exposition in better hands than my own, I set off with my camera and visited all four of the missions the Franciscans had with the Huichols. I had to touch down for a night or two in Tepic between each visit. I was tired before I even started for Jesús María.

The flight to Jesús María was as spectacular as the flight to Santa Clara, but the landing was not high in the cool fragrance of the pines but on a sandy strip on the flats down by a river, where the heat wrapped me up like a hot blanket. I was trying hard to get over being so spoiled, but this heat was more than I had bargained for.

I said a forlorn good–bye to Padre Jacinto. He was not only the director of the Santa Clara mission, but also the pilot of the mission plane. He was the only Franciscan in the Sierra whom I had had a chance to know.

As he spun the little plane around and tipped it on its side to negotiate the narrow canyon on the far side of the mountain, a small, rotund man materialized at my side, a burro beside him.

"Taxi?" he asked jauntily, tying my bags on the burro's back. I trudged up the path behind him, up the hill covered with dead, gray underbrush that smelled of dust. I wanted out.

The church, when the rotund man, the bishop, the burro, and I reached it, looked enormous, looming as it did over the little adobe houses. Its walls were of mud and a meter thick. Its high–vaulted roof was miraculously intact, and its square, crenellated towers looked new, but the white paint on its broad, flat facade was peeling, and the wall itself was pitted.

The bishop's house, the curato, where I would have to ask asylum, was pasted along one side of the church and protruded forward to make, with the church, two sides of a sandy atrium. The other two sides were enclosed by a rough stone wall.

As we stood there in the atrium for a moment, a modishly dressed girl, a mestiza (that's to say, like most Mexicans, mostly Spanish but with some Indian blood), swaggered arrogantly up the path between the old church and the new government school across the way. She was balancing on her head a pink plastic washtub full of wet dishes. She swiveled her neck to give us a haughty stare and then swaggered on.

"She was washing the dishes in the river," the bishop explained.

Across the gravelly road in front of the atrium were buildings almost as old as the church and fully as abused. One had a covered sidewalk with a stone bench against the wall. Seated on it, like birds on a wire, were five Cora Indians in their big white hats, their white muslin trousers tied at the ankle, and their long–sleeved shirts of magenta, green, purple, orange, and peacock blue. They looked across at us with dark, incurious eyes.

The girl turned to the right and disappeared on the far side of the school.

"The mestizos live upriver," the bishop said.

I had seen from the air, flying in, that it was so. On a long, narrow shelf on the side of the mountain, the little tile roofs were lined up, side by side, for perhaps a mile on both sides of a road leading up from the church. The river was a blue ribbon down below.

"The Coras live downriver," the bishop said, and that, too, I had seen from the air. The houses seemed just like the mestizos' except that some of them were larger, and although they started out sedately on the sides of two lanes, they seemed to be placed any which way where the land widened out in the curve of the river below.

"We here at the church are right in the middle," the bishop said. And so it was.

The burro was standing stolidly, but its owner was fidgeting. The time had come when I really had to ask the bishop for shelter.

It took all my courage to do so. I had no invitation. I was not a Catholic. I had photographed the bishop the second time I was in Santa Clara, and he didn't remember me. I shouldn't have come.

The bishop was a large man with a dark, kind face and a deep, serious voice. His bare feet were in worn leather sandals, but his long, brown Franciscan habit with its girdle of knotted white rope was immaculate, and he seemed to be quite unaware that there was something majestic about him. I had the distinct feeling that for some reason he disapproved of me, but, with exquisite courtesy, he not only welcomed me into the curato, he brought me a warm bottle of Pepsi and gave me a bed.

It was a very Franciscan bed. The wooden planks rested on the iron trestles they used in church for coffins.

The bishop's house was called the curato because it was supposed to be the house of the presiding priest, the *cura*. Curas came and went, I learned, but the curato was always the home of the bishop.

It was a very Mexican house, the curato, a long, plain patio sur-

bounded on three sides by strings of adobe rooms with doors onto the courtyard. No room opened into any other, except that the kitchen did have a door into the dining room. Most of the rooms were bedrooms with beds like mine. When there were more bodies than beds, a few guests would have to sleep on the floor. An enterprising friar had purloined twenty-three slats to make shelves for a little library.

The patio was unpretentious but inviting, with four spreading trees and with big-leaved tropical plants bursting out of large tin cans set against a scabrous whitewashed wall. There was a bougainvillea in violent pink bloom burgeoning over a rickety pergola in front of the kitchen door. The patio would have been a pleasant place to sit if there had been anything to sit on.

It was unpaved. It had packed earth underfoot except for a few haphazard islands of concrete on which to stub one's toe. A cavernous open cistern provided buckets of water for washing clothes, bathing, and flushing the curato's three toilets. Water for drinking went into big clay urns in the kitchen.

There were four girls living in the curato at the time, doing the cooking, sweeping, and washing of the bishop's laundry. Three of them were mestizas, who gave me a chilly welcome when I presented myself to them. They regarded me with blank eyes and did not even tell me their names. I remembered the hospitality of the Santa Clara mission and shivered.

The fourth girl was a Cora. Even if she hadn't had those three colored combs in her glossy black hair, that pink basque waist, and that flouncy flowered skirt, I would still have known she was a Cora. It wasn't just the bronzy cast of her skin. It was the modeling of her face, just a trifle Asian. The bishop, who had been around the world, said that in Vietnam she would pass as a native. She seemed to me to be a little disdainful, perhaps of the other girls, as well she might be, perhaps of me, the gringa. In either case, she at least told me her name. She said it was Chuy, short for María de Jesús.

Dinner was at two o'clock in the afternoon, served in the dining room with its pockmarked walls, its plastic replica of the Last Supper, its photograph of the pope, and its drugstore calendar. The bishop, large, dark, and benevolent, sat at the head of the table. The rest of us, a couple of workmen who were making benches for the church and a complement of Coras down from their *ranchos*, accommodated ourselves along the sides. Two of the girls ate with us. The other two brought spaghetti and beans to the table in the pots they had been cooked in and kept flipping tortillas on the mud stove in the lean-to attached to the kitchen. We served ourselves with big kitchen spoons. Each of us had an enamel bowl and a metal tablespoon to eat with, but the workmen and the Coras scorned the spoons and scooped up the beans and spaghetti with their tortillas, their edible cutlery.

I went to the Rosary that afternoon and for the first time really saw the church. It was a revelation. The Coras had built it under the supervision of the Jesuits, who had persuaded the Indians to come down from their thatched huts in the mountains to found a town and build a church above the river. None of this I knew that first afternoon. Only that it was almost incredible that Indians so isolated in their mountain fortress could have built a structure so big, so strong, and so enduring. They had started it in the 1600s and finished it in 1723, just forty-four years before the Jesuits were expelled and the Coras were left to practice their own religion, the *costumbre*.

The costumbre centered on the *santitos* in the church. These were the statues of the Holy Family and the Catholic saints that filled the niches up the wall behind the altar and the platforms in front of the recessed windows. Just inside the door, a larger-than-life statue of Christ had a wig of human hair and exposed ribs of real bones.

The Franciscans had been in Jesús María only some fifteen years. The church and the santitos still belonged to the Indians. The Rosary, however, seemed to be attended exclusively by mestizos.

I slipped into the church as inconspicuously as I could, a little late, and sat down in back. In front of me there was just one black hump after another, the heads and shoulders of the mestizas covered with their speckled black jersey *rebozos*, the long, straight shawls many wore whenever they left their houses, or with the black lace mantillas they called, I learned later, *mananitas*. I was acutely conscious that my own head was bare. Two old men who came in later than I did looked at me sharply as they passed by me to take their places on the left side of the aisle. Having been brought up to believe it was bad form to be conspicuous, I made up my mind to buy a rebozo if I could find one.

In the aisle, a little girl, perhaps a year old, was playing with a pair of red nylon underpants. Farther down the aisle, two little boys a year or so older were taking turns dropping a peso on its edge and scrambling after it as it clattered away.

After many Hail Marys, the congregation rose and sang. I was appalled. With a Catholic heritage of some of the most beautiful sacred music ever written, why were they droning out this banal, dreary tune, and all in unison? Even if they had sung parts, I decided, and some of the communicants had not been tone deaf, the music would still have been inexpressibly dismal.

The heat was smothering. Two little rivers of sweat ran down my cheeks in front of my ears.

The faithful were still singing when a Cora Indian padded down the aisle. He held his woven bag of red and pink yarn against the breast of his emerald-green shirt. Before the altar, he went down on his two knees, blessed himself with a complicated crossing and recrossing, and apparently prayed for a minute or two. Then he crossed himself again and rose to circle the altar, climb up behind it, and stop in front of the first niche in the wall. The bishop told me later that the santito there was Saint Anthony, the patron saint of herdsmen. The Cora was making offerings for the well-being of his livestock.

He took from his bag a small nosegay of purple flowers and tenderly placed it at one side of the santito. Then he took out a small white disk, held it up in front of Saint Anthony, and carefully laid it at the santito's feet. That done, looking straight ahead, he slipped down and circled the altar, then knelt to cross himself and pray again before he padded up the aisle and out of the big open door.

The congregation was back on its knees by now, and soon the Rosary was over. I waited in my seat as the women filed out from their places on the right side of the aisle. Their glances at me were not admiring. It appeared that I was the only woman in Jesús María wearing pants.

Back in the curato, I sought out the girls.

"The women were all wearing skirts," I said anxiously.

"The bishop disapproves of women in trousers," Chuy, the Cora girl, said blandly.

Now I knew why he disapproved of me.

Where could I buy some material to make a skirt? I asked. And a rebozo?

The mestiza girls eyed me impassively and said nothing. Chuy told me that there was a kind of a shop up the broad gravel strip across from the church. I slunk out to find it.

My camera proved to be useless. The Coras permitted nobody to take pictures inside the church and did not choose to be photographed themselves, not even Chuy. This I regretted exceedingly, as the women were even more decorative than the men.

They looked as if they had taken their cut from a Victorian fashion magazine: a tight bodice of poplin in some outrageous color and a wide, flouncing skirt in a wildly exuberant print, always in a contrasting hue. The blouse had a little cloth ruffle half a foot out from the high neck at the top and a little peplum down below. Both blouse and skirt were trimmed with bias tape and rickrack, preferably in a color that did not appear elsewhere in the costume. With three colored combs in the back of their shiny black hair, the women were truly spectacular.

They carried their babies on their backs in slings made of their black rebozos tied on over one shoulder and under the other arm.

In place of photographing the extra-photogenic Coras, I was reduced to snapping pictures of the mestiza girls inside the curato. Their disposition toward me improved from the attention I gave them, but they eventually got as bored as I was.

Then Padre Domingo bounced in from a tour of the ranchos on his ugly little dun-colored mule, and life in Jesús María was never dull again.

2

Well and Truly Roped In

*P*adre Domingo was a charismatic young Franciscan priest with an infectious three-cornered grin, a tendency to freckle, and an incurable habit of hugging children. The grubbier the children were, the harder he hugged them. As he scrambled off his mule, three children were hopping beside it waiting to be hugged.

"What are you doing here?" he asked, grinning over the head of the first child who assaulted him.

"Nothing," I said.

"I'll fix that," he said, and he did.

Padre Domingo had a speaking acquaintance with medicine and a burning desire to heal. He also had cartons and cartons of second-hand medicine donated by believers who, on cleaning out their medicine chests, gave the leftovers to the missions. Much of the medicine was perfectly good, but the padre didn't know what it was for. He put me to work to find out.

At one side of the covered entrance into the patio through which the burros carried water for the cistern, there was an enormous room off by itself. It was not only huge but also lofty, and it had such wide cracks in its raw adobe walls that only Franciscans would have faith enough to trust it to hold together through a heavy rain. It served for catechism classes, company dinners, and lottery games. Off in one corner it housed a few medicines in a rickety cabinet, a splintery table, and a shaky homemade chair that always got requisitioned if the bishop had invited one too many Coras for dinner.

This was Padre Domingo's clinic. Here, with the help of an antiquated pharmaceutical dictionary, I began to label in Spanish: "Cough. 1 teaspoon every four hours." "Rheumatism. Danger. Look in the book." Anything at or near expiration date, I threw away.

There was a government Health Center in Jesús María, a pretty little building with an outdoor office covered with a tile roof and an exuberant pink bougainvillea. The center housed a medical-school graduate doing his required year of social service, if one was available, and enjoyed the services of a permanent male nurse, Don Serafim. The budding doctors came and went, doing their duty laxly or conscientiously depending on their bringing up and then leaving gratefully to complete their education in a hospital before starting to earn money for their services.

Don Serafim was there for life. He was a crotchety middle-age bachelor who had doctored Coras and mestizos alike for years before there had been a Health Center or *médico* in town. He had a smooth, bland face blending into a smooth large bald spot over which he carefully combed a few strands of long hair from the left side to the right. He treated all his patients as if they were his children, beloved but naughty. He clumped around the Health Center peering down throats and giving shots, scolding. It was said that the night he had to take twenty stitches in the scalp of the man from La Guerra who had been attacked with a broken bottle, he berated not only the victim, but also the girl teacher who was holding the flashlight. He had a beautiful voice, a sweet true baritone, and when he sang, even the banal music in Mass sounded lovely.

When I first discovered that Padre Domingo was dispensing medicine without a prescription and that there was a medical-school graduate in town, I reacted as would any other law-abiding U.S. citizen: I was horrified. Then I discovered that the Health Center and Padre Domingo were on the best of terms, and I was baffled, but I kept right on labeling.

Padre Domingo, never one to miss a golden opportunity, put me to other tasks: boiling hypodermic syringes, massaging swollen knees with a sticky mixture of peyote and alcohol, cleaning and bandaging wounds.

I forgot all about taking pictures for the exposition in the pleasure of doing something that seemed immediately useful. The little plane flew in and out again, and I went down to the airstrip only to salute Padre Jacinto. There were two Huichol students living in my house on the fringe of Guadalajara. I trusted them to take care of everything at home.

Pretty soon I began helping with the sick children who were brought into the clinic. Having taken care of my own before the days of immunization for measles, whooping cough, and the like, I had a certain diagnostical advantage. Our family doctor, back on Long Island, had always said that I ought to have been one and had taught me much more than how to keep a wound from getting infected, so I wasn't a total loss.

Sometimes I tagged along behind the padre to one or another of the dark little adobe houses that lined the cobbled street. Nobody had ever managed to make an ecclesiastical figure out of him, and he trudged through the town with his loose white cut–off pants flapping around his calves, a stained brown shirt, and a completely disreputable straw hat. The people loved him for it.

Sometimes he would let me trudge behind him up the easier trails on visits to the little adobe houses in the mountains round-about. I watched with disbelief as he gave shots of penicillin to a baby with mosquito bites, with admiration as he supported the head of an aged woman so she could drink her cinnamon tea, and with forbearance as he hugged the children.

Little by little, I began to know the people, to know which were the light–skinned Coras and which the dark–skinned mestizos. I began to have a few acquaintances: Coras whose indifference began to change to a prickly kind of familiarity, mestizos whose suspiciousness began to change to a tentative kind of friendliness. Sometimes I would slip out of the curato by myself to stroll down one of the two cobbled streets, early in the morning, relishing the sweet, spicy smell of the torch pine with which the fires had just been lighted in the flat mud stoves. Sometimes I would meet with someone I recognized. Often the person would not only return my greeting, but also would stop and solemnly shake my hand.

Once or twice, I had the luck to come upon a Cora woman making one of the beautiful woven bags I had so loved to sell in the exposition. She would sit on the ground, the small back loom attached at one end to a tree and at the other end to her by a cord around her waist. The wool would be of two colors, one for the background and one for the figures of birds, jaguars, flowers, or involved geometrics. The most beautiful of the bags were of hand-spun wool from the backs of one white sheep and one black one. The showiest were those of boughten yarn in two bright colors: orange and pink, blue and green. Once I had the luck to see a woman setting up her pattern. She was sitting on the ground behind a lineup of slender wooden wands thrust into the ground, winding the yarn between them, so intent on her design that she didn't even notice I was watching.

Little by little, I began to discover Jesús María. I found that it was far from repulsive, as I had thought at the start. I discovered that it was beautiful. The few trees in the town, some of them strange to me, were beautiful. The river, snaking its way down below the town, was slow and sluggish, but it was blue and beautiful. I was amazed.

The nights, too, were beautiful, with the sky a black, star-spangled blanket.

I discovered that the church, which was, as the bishop said, right in the middle, was actually the heart of the town. It was never closed. At midnight one could see through the big open doors to the candles flickering on the handsome old altar, the one where the priests had celebrated Mass with their backs to the congregation before the new laws of the Church required them to face the faithful and a plain new altar had been installed in front of the old one. Coras slipped into the church at any hour of the day or night to pad down the aisle, climb up behind the old altar, and leave their offerings at the feet of the santitos in the niches in the wall. Sometimes an aged Cora, tall and slender, would be standing against the wall to the left of the altar, his arms crossed on his chest, his fine, chiseled face absolutely expressionless.

"It's Don Nazario," Padre Domingo told me. "They call him the bishop of the Coras. He knows all there is to know about the costumbre and supervises its observance."

Often a couple of mestizas, their black rebozos shrouding their heads and shoulders, would sit on one of the front benches for an hour or so.

"What are they doing there, Chuy?" I asked.

"Visiting," Chuy said.

"Visiting?"

"Visiting the Virgin," Chuy said, pitying my ignorance.

The fun of the town centered on the church, too: volleyball in the atrium, baseball outside, carnivals at night with girls selling *pozole* and boys breaking confetti–filled eggshells on innocent skulls. A woman named Chela, whom I came to know well, always sold Chocomilk: one peso for a paper cup of Chocomilk plain, two pesos for a cup of Chocomilk with a tablespoon of potable alcohol added.

So many of my friends from the States were so convinced that the Church exploited the poor that I expected that somebody would pass the plate at every Mass, and so I attended the first one with money in my pocket. I discovered that a collection was taken only on Sundays, when the mestizos, in a burst of generosity, would drop a coin worth forty cents in U.S. money into the basket. The money went out of the curato, not into it.

I presumed that it came from the benefactors who also supported the missions. From my room on the patio, next door to the bishop's, I could hear him pounding his typewriter at midnight and at dawn, asking, I am sure, for help.

During the day when he was not celebrating Mass or plodding down The Street in Front of the Church in his hot brown Franciscan habit to visit a sick Cora, he would be typing, typing, typing in his room. Coras, and sometimes mestizos, would come to the burros' entrance asking to see him. I would loop back through the long patio to his room. He would look caged for a moment and then, with his usual courtesy, would say, "Send them in."

Then he would listen to them as if he had nothing else to do all day. Sometimes they came only for counsel. Sometimes they were desperate for money, and the bishop would give them what he could.

I had never known such a completely selfless man. I was pleased to discover, though, that he was not without humor.

"A woman came to me today," I told him. "A Cora. She said her grandmother had died and they had no money to buy a box. I gave her a few pesos."

The bishop smiled.

"I did, too," he said. "But I think you should know that her grand–mother dies every year."

The most arresting discovery I made was that Jesús María was Mexico upside down, at least as far as this gringa's preconceptions were concerned. The land belonged not to the mestizos but to the Indians, the whole big Cora zone. Mestizos could build houses, even fence in cornfields, but the land under the houses and inside the fences belonged to the tribe, and it was prudent for a mestizo to get permission to build or to fence.

The government was not in the hands of the mestizos. Jesús María was the capital of the *municipio*, the Mexican municipios being the governmental units of which a state is composed. Our municipio took in the whole big Cora zone. The Presidente Municipal, the elected chief executive, was a Cora. So were the judge and all the other important officials. There were two mestizos working in the ancient government building, the Presidencia, but they were hirelings.

The school was not run by mestizos. There were two mestizas from Tepic, pretty young teachers doing their compulsory year of social service, but the superintendent of schools was a Cora. The principal was a Cora. All the important teachers were Coras. I was fascinated.

During that spring in Jesús María, the weather was at its most unbearable, blisteringly hot in the daytime, almost as hot at night. The dirty, burning wind stung my face when I ventured outside and left a thick brown film on everything indoors. I woke up in the morning with a gritty skin.

All the same, I wanted to know Jesús María better.

The bishop, who had forgiven me my slacks as soon as I abandoned them, was hospitable beyond imagining, but I could not impose further on his kindness. I rented a little house from Chela, the woman of the Chocomilk, telling myself that if I could stick it out for a month I would stay for a year.

It was July when I returned to Jesús María after my monthly English-speaking respite in Guadalajara. I brought with me what I would need for the most primitive kind of living: sheets, towels, a couple of pots, some spoons and dishes, and a one-burner kerosene stove that smoked. I moved into my little house and began to try to learn to live like a native while I kept on working for Padre Domingo in the curato.

The rains had already started. The world was beginning to turn green and to smell of mud. Tiny red velvet bugs scampered over the wet ground between the starting cloverleafs of the peanuts planted on the flats down by the river. It rained every afternoon and into the night. Mornings dawned fresh and delicious, but as soon as the sun came up the whole world began to steam. Pigs wallowed luxuriously in the puddles. Scorpions took refuge inside houses and stung babies. Mosquitoes swarmed in through the windows and bit everyone.

When I left for Guadalajara at the end of that July, I had rented the house for another month and I had a mission. Chela, now my landlady, gave it to me.

"Bring medicine," she told me. "The babies die like flies in August."

"What of?" I asked her.

"*Chorro* and *basca*, the Coritas say," she told me and laughed. "It's the vulgar way to say diarrhea and vomiting. The *vecinos* say '*soltura,*' looseness."

I had already learned that the mestizos were called vecinos. Neighbors. The Indian word for them.

"But why in August?" I persisted.

"Because of the rains. Everything on the mountain washes down to the river."

Outside of the curato and the Health Center, there was almost no drainage in Jesús María. Almost everyone defecated on the side of the mountain. Everybody got their drinking water from holes dug in the sand by the river. Almost nobody boiled water to drink. It was a wonder that only the babies died.

Fired with missionary zeal, I went into action immediately. With the bishop's permission, I made signs and tacked them on the wooden doors of the church and on any other surface that would hold a nail. They said, in Spanish:

BOIL YOUR WATER BEFORE DRINKING

WASH YOUR HANDS BEFORE EATING

AVOID DIARRHEA, SOLTURA, CHORRO

It wasn't until weeks later that I understood why the bishop had seemed amused when I asked his permission or why Chela's husband, Don Paco, had ducked down behind the counter of Chela's store when I had shown the signs to Chela.

Except for the schoolchildren and some of the middle-age Coras, almost nobody in Jesús María could read.

Down in Guadalajara, I made more sense.

I timorously approached my own doctor. Far from being shocked that we were practicing medicine without a license in the curato, he gave me more instruction than I could possibly assimilate. I wrote down what he told me and bought the book he recommended. It was in English, written by specialists on the medical faculties of prestigious U.S. universities. For each disease, it gave the symptoms, the diseases with which it might be confused, its progress, treatment, and medication. It became my bible. A medical student who owned a pharmacy sold me medicine at a discount. I went back to Jesús María better prepared than when I had left.

It was a good thing. The Health Center was closed. The temporary doctor and the permanent male nurse were both on vacation. Padre Domingo was in Mexico City, taking a course in anthropology. I was the only person in Jesús María with medicine and some inkling of what to do with it.

Many of the little houses were closed, their one window filled with adobe bricks, their rough wooden doors padlocked. The families had gone to their ranchos high up in the mountains "to drink milk," they said, to take care of their new calves, and to make cheese. Cattle, the riches of Coras and mestizos alike, were kept on the range, where it was cooler and there was pasture. There, the animals would not die of heat and hunger.

Chela had cousins in the mountains who cared for her animals and Don Paco's. They themselves stayed in Jesús María to keep the store open.

I could go to the few houses of those who stayed in Jesús María, in the daytime dragging myself through the steamy heat, at night sloshing along through the pouring rain, my medicines clutched to my stomach under my old raincoat. The ranchos, however, were far beyond my reach. Some of them were four or five hours away. I had no knowledge of the trails and no mule to carry me over them. Ailing children were thus brought down to me in the arms of their fathers or on the backs of their mothers, down the treacherous tracks that were now little rivers of mud.

August was a month of torrential rains. Every afternoon, the purpling clouds rolled down from the north and drenched but did not cool us. The air, day and night, was like a hot, wet flannel sheet, wrapping us in steam. My sweaty clothes stuck to me as if they had been soaked in honey. Peeling them off for a sponge bath was an exercise for a contortionist, which I was not. Pulling on dry clothes was almost as hard, for I was sweating again by the time I had hung up my towel.

August was also a month of itching. The insects were vicious. If ever I stopped in the shade of a tree or loitered outdoors after the clouds had covered the sun, they attacked me. Tiny gnats hovered around my head. Black flies bit my legs through my stockings. I couldn't wear makeup for the bumblebees.

As if to compensate, August was also a month of flowers. Jesús María and all the wilderness around it burst into bloom, up the mountainsides and down into the *barrancas*, the almost-bottomless canyons. Soft yellow blossoms like big buttercups carpeted the corners of the atrium. Gentle clusters of bright pink flowerlets climbed the cliffs on rambunctious green vines. Indians came down from their ranchos with orchids in their hats.

For me, alone as I was with the only medicine in town, August was a month of suppressed terror.

It wasn't the *granos*, the ugly spreading sores, that scared me. Those I could cure with a foul black concoction that Padre Domingo had brewed before he slipped off to Mexico City.

It wasn't the infected machete cuts. Deep and dangerous as they were, they responded to old-fashioned remedies. With soaks of Epsom salts, wet dressings, and rest, they cured themselves.

What really scared me were the dysentery Chela had warned me of, the salmonella, and shigella infections, which could kill the babies like flies.

On the wall of the big crumbling room where Padre Domingo had his clinic, I pasted a chart I had prepared from the book the doctor had prescribed. It showed the symptoms of simple diarrhea, salmonellosis, shigellosis, amoebiosis, and typhoid fever. It also showed the remedies for each, milligrams of medicine to kilograms of body weight.

The medicine of choice for our chief killers was an antibiotic. I had been conditioned to believe that antibiotics should be given only when prescribed by a doctor. When the choice, however, is between probable recovery and almost certain death, there is no choice. I consulted the chart on the wall, guessed at the victim's weight, and gave the antibiotic.

Not a single baby died, nor any child or grown-up. I was hooked.

3

Learning Magic Takes a Little Time

When Padre Domingo came back from the anthropological course in Mexico City, it was clear that travel had broadened him. He still grinned the same three–cornered grin, he still hugged children indiscriminately, but his attitude toward me was distinctly patronizing.

"You have learned the first half very well, the medicine half," he told me as he softened a sterile bandage with a dirty thumb. "Now you must learn the other half."

"So?"

"Yes. You gave that man pills when he wanted a shot. He wanted a shot, so I gave him one."

Padre Domingo put the bandage down on the table and reached for the Merthiolate. "The man had a cold in the nose. The shot you gave him would have served for double pneumonia. In the United States, we call that killing a fly with a sledge hammer."

"This is not the United States," Padre Domingo reminded me. "These people like shots."

"Why?" I asked him. "Their love of violence or their belief in magic?"

"Magic. You must develop some magic yourself."

"There is such a thing as integrity," I said sanctimoniously.

"Ay, Catareen," the padre said. "You are very American."

The man with the cut foot put on his huarache and hobbled out of the room. The wound was deep, but, in spite of the contaminated bandage, it healed fast.

I stubbornly declined to give shots at the start, even when an illness could have used a medicine that was quicker by muscle than by mouth. The truth was that I was scared to death to give one. I kept practicing on oranges, the way my friend in Guadalajara had taught me, but I remained a thoroughgoing coward.

Padre Domingo, on the other hand, was very brave. With a hypodermic syringe, he was dauntless, and he plunged in antibiotics as if they were sterile water, sometimes, I felt, when they might do more harm than good.

The trust the people, both mestizos and Coras, had in him was fanatical. It was helped, of course, by his being a priest, but it was by no means diminished by an event that the faithful in Jesús María regarded as a miracle.

Shortly before I flew into Jesús María the first time, the budding doctor in the Health Center gave some kind of shot to Doña Alberta, a middle-age mestiza. Doña Alberta walked out of the Health Center and fell to the ground, apparently lifeless. She stopped breathing, and Don Serafim could find no pulse, so he ran, limping, for the priest. Padre Domingo came sprinting. He was prepared to administer the last rites, but first he gave mouth-to-mouth resuscitation, and the woman came to.

"God was helping me," Padre Domingo told me later.

From that time on, it was obvious to almost everyone that the doctor killed and the *padrecito* brought the dead to life. Padre Domingo was so besieged by the sick and wounded that he scarcely had time for his parochial duties. In spite of his cavalier attitude toward germs, to the best of my knowledge all his patients, as if by magic, recovered.

His only competition, really, was from an older kind of magic, the magic practiced by the Cora shamans, the *curanderos*.

I had read a little about the curanderos in the sparse works of anthropologists. I knew that they sang prayers in Cora, that they sucked out sickness and stroked on smoke. I had seen the arrows Padre Domingo had: arrows that the curanderos waved to bless and cure; beautiful, delicate, handmade arrows, dripping with the feathers of tropical birds. I knew that, to a Cora, sickness was a punishment meted out to those who neglected their religious obligations, who failed to make appropriate offerings, not only to the saints in the church, but also to skulls in certain sacred caves, who failed to observe the costumbre. The Cora curandero was the bridge between God and man, and, as such, his prestige was understandably incalculable.

Padre Domingo recognized this and never tried to undermine it. Sometimes he even tried to cure like a curandero, waving his feathered arrows and singing in a high falsetto, to the affectionate merriment of any Coras who witnessed the performance. At least once he managed to work directly with a curandero.

One morning when I was still staying at the curato, he plodded in late for breakfast, looking sleepy and pale. He had spent the night with Felipe, a Cora who had something that looked unpleasantly like cholera.

"It was quite a picture," Padre Domingo said. "There was Don Serafim, trying to give Felipe an I.V. and his veins had collapsed. Don Serafim had to give it subcutaneously, in the belly. Felipe had a swelling there like a soccer ball. And there was the Cora curandero, singing prayers in Cora in the corner, and the Mexican priest giving shots to Felipe and singing prayers in Spanish by the bed. . . ."

"What curandero?" I asked.

"Don Teodulo."

"And he stayed with you there?" I asked incredulously.

Green as I was, I had heard about Don Teodulo. Chuy had told me that Don Teodulo refused to cure anyone who got mixed up with modern medicine.

"Oh, he tried to leave," Padre Domingo said, "but I persuaded him to stay. 'Please don't go,' I said. 'We need all the help we can get.' So he stayed and stayed, and we both sang and sang. Different prayers, of course, but at the same time."

Padre Domingo volunteered my services to sit with Felipe all that morning up on the mesa of San Miguel, watching the drip from a bottle hanging from a rafter. Felipe's veins would now accept the intravenous hydration.

He was on a native bed, a mat of Mexican bamboo on supports made of tree limbs smoothed with a machete. The floor was of soft black dirt, the roof blackened tile. The house was very old and, like so many on the mesa, was not of adobe but of rough brown rocks with mud and pebble fill. There were gunnysacks of corn on the floor and, in the corner, hand-woven woolen bags hanging on deer antlers suspended from the roof. Felipe's mother was cooking over three stones at the far end of the big lofty room. A little light filtered in through the doorless opening on the side of the house.

Felipe and I talked. I asked about Don Teodulo. "He's a priest, of course," I said.

"No. He's a doctor."

"But he prays," I said.

"Of course he prays. We don't want to die. He prays to God not to take us away, not to let us die. He's a doctor."

"Did he suck after the padre left?"

Felipe put his fist to his mouth and sucked noisily. Then he laughed.

"Yes, he sucked."

"What did he find?"

"Oh, just some rocks and things."

He laughed again. Then he looked at me.

"All the same, you can't see anything in his hand before he sucks," he said, confidentially.

After I moved into my little house, I began to have more friends among the Coras. One of them was Micaela, a tall, handsome young woman married to a devout young man of the tribe, devout to the costumbre, that is. He came to me at midnight to ask me to go to see her because she was sick.

She was on a native bed in the cavernous room, the only room in the house. From the light of a spirit lamp improvised from an insecticide can, I could just see the feathered arrow thrust into the brown rock wall to protect the house from harm. Micaela thanked me for coming.

"A señor came, too," she said.

"Don Teodulo?"

"Yes. In the early morning. He stayed all day. He sucked out two corncobs this long."

"With the kernels still on them?"

"Of course." She looked at me soberly.

"One doesn't get better with your medicine alone," she said. "We need both. Your medicine and the other, too. Do you have this custom in your own country?"

"No. We don't."

"Well, my sister died of just having your kind of medicine. She got stiff, like this [demonstrating], and died. One needs both," she said again.

Sucking as they did and then displaying rocks, corncobs, and the like, the curanderos, I was convinced, were accomplished artists at sleight of hand. All the same, I respected them. I felt that there must be something deeply consoling about their ministrations, so personal, so prolonged. I thought that Micaela could be right, that the Coras probably did fare better when they had both our kind of medicine and their own.

I wondered if I would ever have a chance to work with a curandero myself. Not like Padre Domingo. I was no priest to sing prayers in any language. Not with Don Teodulo. From what Chuy had told me, I was sure he was too important. But there must be humbler curanderos. Perhaps one of them would let me work with him, would let me cure my way while he cured his.

But how was I to meet a curandero?

The answer came sooner than I had expected. Mateo, a fine, gentle young Cora with the face of a saint, came to my window early one morning asking for help. He had brought his little daughter down from the rancho in a coma. She had had a soaring fever in the mountains and had then gone into a sleep from which nobody could awaken her. She was a beautiful little girl, four or five, Mateo wasn't sure.

With some difficulty, I persuaded the budding médico in the Health Center to visit her. He had insisted that the child be taken to the Health Center. Mateo had refused to comply. Finally, the doctor-to-be did go with me to the windowless house, where the child lay on the native bed. All her relations were there, cooking on the mud stove, sitting on the floor, standing beside her bed, praying softly in Cora. The doctor examined her.

"I can't do anything for her," he said. "Take her to Tepic."

"*Sabe*," Mateo said, which apparently meant "Who knows?" but was actually a polite way of saying, "Don't be ridiculous." Mateo had no intention of removing his little daughter, whom he loved, from all the supernatural forces in Jesús María, the saints in the church, the skulls in the cave, the curandero.

The médico shrugged, left the child in my care, and went back to the Health Center, refusing to have anything more to do with the little girl.

She woke up. Her fever soared, and, every time I lowered it a little, she went into convulsions. Then she drifted off into a deep sleep from which nobody could awaken her.

I was frantic. Padre Domingo was away, and I was very new. I read and read, but I didn't know where to look in the book my own doctor had prescribed. I kept going back every few hours to the house with timid doses of antibiotics in watery solutions. I spooned milk made from powder into her little mouth every time I went to see her. At night, I would have to step over bodies sleeping on the floor to reach her bed.

I came upon the curandero there with the little girl early one morning. It was the second time she had been in a coma. Her father, mother, and grandmother were holding her in a sitting position while the curandero blew smoke into his hand and stroked her back with it.

He was a young Cora, this curandero, intent, serious, dedicated, close to exhaustion. I knew he had been there all night because twice when I had come to the house he was singing inside so I hadn't come in. I watched from just inside the door until he had finished and had stored his instruments in his box of woven palm: his feathered arrows, his ceremonial pipe, his sucking tube. Then I spoke to him.

"I hope we can work together," I said respectfully.

He regarded me blandly for a moment. Then he picked up his box, said something in Cora to the family, and slipped out of the house as silently as a cat.

The little girl died. I expected Mateo to blame me, or the doctor-to-be, or even the curandero, but the whole family blamed nobody but themselves. They were convinced that God had taken the little girl because they had neglected their religious obligations, the costumbre.

I timidly asked if they would like me to go with them to bury her.

"Of course," Mateo said. "You were with us all the time."

Such sweetness after such tragedy was too much for me. I cried.

A week or so later, I heard some ugly news: the doctor-to-be was out to get me. He had said, Chela told me, that he was writing to the chief of the government Health Department in Tepic, telling him that an American woman was giving free medicine in Jesús María. I was scared. In the United States, it would be illegal. I wouldn't be able to give anyone medicine there even if the person would die if I didn't. How was it here in Mexico? Was I breaking a law? What would they do with me if I was? Arrest me? Deport me? Forbid me to prescribe another aspirin?

I didn't have to wait long to find out. Here they came, two purposeful young men, both in what looked like uniforms.

"May we come in?" they wanted to know.

"Please do," I said without a quaver. "Won't you sit down?"

They had already sat down on my bed.

And to what did I owe the honor of their visit?

"We've been up in the ranchos," the older one said. "They tell us you give them medicine."

"That's true," I said. "I do."

"Well," he said, "they seem to have so much more faith in you than in the doctor that we have come to ask you to work with us, as a member of the National Commission for the Eradication of Malaria."

"Of course," I heard myself saying. "What do I do?"

"Take care of the victims. The government supplies the medicine, but first you must make blood smears to send to the laboratory in Tepic for diagnosis."

Blood smears!

"Blood smears? But I'm not a nurse. I don't know how."

"We know that," the younger man said. "We're here to teach you." And he proceeded to lay out on the bed equipment, and medicine, and sheaves of printed instructions.

So I gave my hand to have my finger pricked for the drop of blood. I had no idea that I was making a commitment that I would be honoring for years and years—or that, in a very few days, the laboratory would be teaching me to diagnose with my own microscope.

Of course, there was still the chief of the Health Department. He did fly out in the showy government plane. I was terrified, but he hadn't come to take me away with him. He had come to take away the doctor-to-be, whom we never saw again.

This interval had been fairly hair-raising for me, but there were always bloody toes to bandage, babies with croup, and polluted water to worry about. No curandero appeared, eager to work with me. And always there, taunting me, was Padre Domingo's brand of magic. At last, of course, I had to come to terms with that.

I naturally realized, from the start, that the psychological effect of his shots had to be dramatic—the innocent flourish with which he filled the hypodermic; the murderous needle; the flash of pain—but I myself only gave practice shots to oranges pilfered from the bishop's one tree, until one moonless night. I was walking home to my little house, following the beam of my flashlight, when Chuy came running through the darkness calling to me.

"Have you any antitoxin, Señora Cata? A baby has been stung by a scorpion."

Behind Chuy, running, too, was a Cora woman with a baby wrapped in her black rebozo. The baby was trying to scream. With every breath, it forced out a strangled, inhuman bark.

We ran all the way to Padre Domingo's clinic. Nothing but a shot would save the child. Mine were the only hands handy. The doctor and Don Serafim were both in Tepic. Padre Domingo was in goodness-knows-what rancho.

Steeling myself as for a major operation, I lighted the lamp, cleaned my hands and the little saw with alcohol, opened the flap on the tiny flask of powder, sawed off the tip of the ampoule without slicing a finger, filled the syringe from the ampoule, squirted the liquid into the flask of powder, and said in what I hoped was a calm, even tone, "Lend me the little buttock."

Just as I had been taught and had practiced so often, I swabbed the appropriate site, stabbed the needle in, and slowly pushed down the plunger. The baby was so numb all over it didn't even feel the shot. It just kept on barking as before.

The shot really was magic. I spent the night on the table in my sleeping bag, but it wasn't really necessary.

The mother walked for an hour or two with the baby in her arms, whispering to it softly in Cora. Then she, too, lay down on the floor on the quilt I had filched from the storeroom. By midnight, the mother and baby were both sleeping peacefully. The baby, so near death when the mother came running, in the morning was drinking coffee and refusing milk.

The baby's bottom was nothing at all like an orange. I didn't enjoy a bit plunging a needle into it, but I had a premonition as I did so that my days of rebellion were over–that from now on I was going to be a slave to the magic of that wicked little hypodermic needle, just like Padre Domingo. I still hoped that I would find a curandero to work with, or, better still, that a curandero would find me.

4

A New Way to Lose Your Shirt

*L*iving in Chela's little house, away from the protection of the curato, took getting used to.

It was really a very little house, only two small rooms at the end
of Chela's compound. It fronted on a gravel strip euphemistically
called The Street of San Miguel, a continuation of the lava flow down
the side of the mesa of San Miguel.

The mesa of San Miguel, where I had sat watching the drip of the
I.V., was the Cora stronghold. Up there was the Casa Fuerte, the
Strong House, the council house of the Cora tribal government.
Down below where we were was still Cora territory, and Chela's
house was one of the few mestiza houses in the Cora part of town.
The Street of San Miguel was the main thoroughfare from the mesa to
the center of Jesús María.

Coras constantly passed my house on their way from San Miguel
to Chela's store or on down the hill to the church. More than one
sloped up to my window, rested his arms on the sill, and examined
the room with dark, appraising eyes. Those I didn't already know
from working in Padre Domingo's clinic asked me where I came from.
All of them asked how much I had paid for my clock.

My house backed onto Chela's patio, a long, gravelly obstacle
course from the wall at my end to the gate in the wall at the other. It
was littered with buckets, washtubs, and huge tin cans and was alive
with hens. The buckets and washtubs were full of water. The cans were
bursting with brawny plants: rosebushes, ferns, lilies, bougainvilleas.

The ubiquitous hens were of three different kinds, all of them weird. There were hens with long, naked, red necks, which I thought at first were diseased. There were hens with fluffy, downy topknots. Weirdest of all, there were hens with feathers that curled out at the tips, giving them a frivolous, flirtatious look. There was also a big white rooster, which chased all the hens indiscriminately and gave the clarion call throughout the night to start all the other cocks in town crowing at the appointed hours.

The only four-footed residents of the patio were a couple of surly yellow dogs, owing to a sign on the outside of the gate that read: "Shut me. Pigs enter."

Strung along the sides of the patio were most of the rooms of Chela's house, rooms like those of the curato, with no windows, one door opening onto the patio, and no doors between rooms. On my side of the patio was Chela's store, the most important part of the compound, as Chela was first and last a merchant. The store had been her father's, and he had left it to her when he died.

Chela was not really pretty. Everything about her was a little too generous: her nose, her mouth, her figure. Her vivacity made up for what she lacked in conventional beauty, and her smile was incandescent. Always at her most ingratiating when she was driving the hardest bargain, she presided behind the makeshift counter in the narrow little store, shamelessly coquetting with her customers as she pressed upon them everything from children's clothes, loose sugar, flashlight batteries, store cookies, lassos, kerosene, pots and pans, soft drinks, cosmetics, and machetes to huaraches and lollipops. Commercial as she was, she could be open handed, too. To the mothers of her ninety-six godchildren, most of them Indians, she doled out armloads of gifts: skirt lengths of bright printed cotton, black jersey rebozos, hand lotion, and powdered milk.

To me she was amused mentor, kind landlady, and, eventually, affectionate friend.

The two rooms in my little house, unlike the other rooms lining the patio, had an opening between them. I also had two doors, one onto the patio and the other onto the so-called street. Both of the doors and the opening between the two rooms had doorsills nearly a foot high and door frames topped off on a level with my ear. To avoid injury, I had to step high and duck low. The first time I entered to take possession of the house, I stubbed my toe on the doorsill and bumped my head hard on the frame.

As soon as my vision cleared, I could see how Chela had decorated the house in honor of my coming.

She had hung holy pictures on the walls, along with a flight of china birds and a wall vase with faded paper flowers in it. In the opening between the two rooms, she had strung up a limp cotton curtain printed with pink roses. She had draped my cupboard, two wooden crates one on top of the other, with a white cloth embroidered in red and green and edged with ball fringe.

The rest of the furnishings were plain.

She had given me a metal table advertising Coca-Cola, two Pepsi Cola chairs, and a shaky wooden contraption with a pole for hanging my clothes. She had scrubbed the brick floor with soap so that it shone and had the clean smell of wet putty.

The bed she had given me was the Mexican equivalent of an army cot, and I stretched out on it gratefully the first night I was in residence.

I had had a hard day.

At six o'clock that morning, I was waiting for the commercial plane in the shack that then served Tepic as the airport building. I had given up flying in the mission plane, not wanting to add my weight to its cargo. I figured that two gunnysacks of beans were worth more in the Sierra than I was.

The commercial plane, a sturdy Beechcraft, did not board us until noon, having serviced various other settlements in the Sierra before flying back to Tepic and taking off for Jesús María. It landed half an hour later, not on the short gravel strip on the flats by the river but on the longer gravel strip on top of the mountain, up at El Cerro. The Coras, hacking away with pick and shovel for minimum government wages, had now finished a terrifying one-lane dirt road, cut out of the sides of the mountains, from El Cerro down to the cliff on the far side of the river from Jesús María.

I had the luck, with two other passengers, to get a ride down to the river in the government's Datsun pickup truck. (It replaced one, I learned later, that had rolled down into the barranca when the Coras were still carving out the road.) José, the dapper young driver from

Tepic, hurtled down the rutted, rocky road, skidding around the hair-
pin curves on the brink of precipices. We arrived, trembling, at the
river, on the wrong side. We could see Jesús María stretched out on its
ledge over the flats, the big white church looming over the little
adobe houses. It seemed very far away. The mountain sheered up behind it, green, green, green.

The road ended at the top of the cliff. The river was far below. It
was very wide and deep now. There was no bridge. We crossed in the
canastilla.

The canastilla was a wooden box with two seats in it, facing each
other. It was suspended from a cable high above the river. You
climbed a short ladder to get into the box, and a strong man with a
grapple hitched the canastilla across on its cable to the other side of
the river, dizzyingly below.

We had to wait half an hour, because the canastilla was on the far
side of the river, and the man with the grapple wasn't expecting us
and had to be looked for. He finally appeared, waved to us, climbed
up into his seat in the wooden box, and hitched the canastilla across
on its cable to our side of the river. We climbed aboard with my luggage and lurched back to the shaky platform on the Jesús María side.

There I waited again. I had early discovered that in Mexico it is
prudent to learn to enjoy waiting, but the sun was hot, the earth was
steaming from last night's rain, a bumblebee was examining my city
makeup, and after fifteen minutes I was very glad to see the approach
of Pancho, Chela's little nephew, with Chela's lop-eared burro. Pancho rescued my bags and boxes and escorted me up the hill to the
house.

Chela was waiting for me with a good assortment of her nu-
merous family. There was her sister Inez, the eldest, with her two
daughters, Alma and Luz. There was her sister Juana, Pancho's
mother, with her daughter, Gloria, and her other little son, Filemon.
There was Arcelia with her two sons, Felipe and Julian, and her
daughter, another Luz. Except for Pancho and Filemon, all the nieces
and nephews were in their early teens.

Chela embraced me enthusiastically. Her sisters embraced me
formally. I had met them all beforehand and came to know them
well. They were all charming, but they paled a little beside Chela's

robust exuberance, her flashing smile. Their children shook hands with me, most of them tentatively. Don Paco, Chela's husband, tall, quite handsome, and very self-possessed, saluted with a smile only faintly roguish.

After the required pleasantries, I stored my few belongings and stumbled down to the curato. Clouds were piling up in the northern sky, great white puffs like scoops of ice cream against the hard blue sky. I hoped I could get home before it began to rain.

At the curato, I paid my respects to the bishop and reported to Padre Domingo. He, with a companionable grin, put me to work repairing a dirty foot with a torn-off toenail. By the time I could start home, the sun was going down. The clouds had slid off to the east and were disappearing behind mountains. The western sky was blazing like a sheet of polished copper. This night there would be no rain.

After a few crackers and some milk made with Chela's boiled water and powder from a can (the can was labeled "*leche entera de vaca en polvo*," which I translated as "whole milk of powdered cow"), I was glad to slip between the sheets on my narrow canvas bed.

The window was open and had no screen. With the darkness came the mosquitoes. They floated in through the window singing. Then something else floated in. A smell. A rank, weedy smell. A stink. When I could stand it no longer, I struggled off the cot. The window had an inside shutter. I closed it tight.

The cot collapsed as I got back on it, but after I had extricated myself I managed to right it again and once more composed myself to sleep. I was just drifting off, exhausted, when I was startled awake by a cry of agony issuing down from the hill behind the house.

"Aaaah. Aaaah. Aaaah."

I quailed. The cries continued.

Should I get up, get dressed, and go out into the dark with my flashlight, searching for a trail up that hill through the deserty shrubs with their spikes, thorns, and needles? Would I get lost? Would I meet up with a scorpion? A snake?

But somebody was in trouble up there, I told myself sternly. Was I a coward?

I was. I stayed in bed.

I confessed to Chela in the morning. It stretched my Spanish a little, but she understood instantly when I quavered, "Aaaah. Aaaah. Aaaah." She laughed.

"It was the old goat," she said, "the one with the bell."

I had seen him at sunset. He had appeared in front of my window with his harem, a handsome white goat with a haughty, accusing eye. I had opened the door to admire him, and he had given me one quick, dirty look and whisked off toward the lava flow, his ladies frisking behind him.

My education was beginning. I had not been acquainted with goats before.

I told Chela about the smell, too.

"Ah, yes," Chela said, "the calabash tree. There's one just up the hill from your house. It's in bloom now. The flowers have a filthy smell. Filthy. There's a story about it. Would you like to hear?"

"*Como no*," I said. "I certainly would."

"Well," Chela said, "they say that the Devil wanted to sit under the calabash tree, it gives such a nice shade. But the calabash tree wouldn't let him. So the Devil gave the flowers that filthy smell to punish the tree. God was sorry for the tree, though. He made the leaves in the shape of a cross, so the Devil can't come near anymore."

Don Paco smiled. He was helping behind the counter. He often smiled when Chela spoke. He was obviously in love with Chela, and she with him. They were both nearly forty but only recently married. Chela's father had forbidden her to marry until after his death, and he had lived a long time.

I made a little detour on my way to Padre Domingo's clinic that morning to see the calabash tree. It was a huge spreading tree with a maze of branches prickled with tiny, deep green leaves. Its big, yellow–ochre blossoms were freakishly attached not to its branches but to its gnarly trunk and the undersides of its heavy limbs. The flowers didn't smell as bad in the morning as they had at night. There was shade enough under the tree for a whole family of devils, and the little leaves were, indeed, in the form of a cross.

Living in the curato, I had learned how much one can happily do without: newspapers, gas stoves, ice, telephones, or any other device for communicating beyond the range of a shout. I still missed the

luxury of water from a faucet, but at the curato, at least, there was al–
ways plenty of water in the cistern. At Chela's it was different.

Chela's water came up from the river on her lop–eared burro. It
patiently made several trips every morning, with Pancho switching it
from behind and occasionally encouraging it further with a kick or
two.

Pancho's nine–year–old brother, Filemon, brought mine to me,
four bucketfuls every morning before school. He dug a hole in the
sand by the river and scooped into my buckets the water that seeped
into the hole. He made two trips, each trip with two buckets swaying
from his shoulder yoke as he trudged up the hill to my house.

For drinking, I boiled some of the water on my smoky kerosene
stove. The rest I used more than once, first for rinsing my supper
dishes, then for bathing, then for washing my clothes.

The problem was that I didn't have enough water to rinse my
clothes properly, and I began to itch almost as much from the de–
tergent as from Jesús María's entomological population. Chela took
pity on me. She undertook to teach me to wash my clothes clean and
rinse them properly, Jesús María style.

With a lime–green plastic washtub of soiled clothes on her head,
she led me down to the river: down the rocky road to the trail down
to the flats, over the flats to the *guamuchil* tree, and then on to the
sandy little beach, downriver from where I had seen Chuy and one of
the mestizas washing the bishop's clothes.

The river was fast and smoke colored from the rains. The bottom
was studded with big invisible stones. On the far side of the river, the
mountain was newly, freshly green with clouds piling up above it in
the blue, blue sky. It was beautiful.

Chela took off her dress, pulled her half–slip up over her ample
breasts, took off her brassiere from underneath, and began to wash
clothes, standing in the river and slapping towels, shirts, dresses, and
underwear on a rough stone that protruded above the water.

I wanted to wash my clothes, but I was timid. In the shade of the
guamuchil tree, there were three Cora men with long wooden
crochet hooks making their fishnets. "Don't bother about them,"
Chela told me. "They're not interested in us."

Upstream, perhaps a city block from us, another Cora man was sitting in the river, the water up to his neck. He glanced at us and glanced away.

I undressed as Chela had done and felt my way over the stones and mud out to a big, flat-topped rock just washed over by a thin flow of water. With the cake of soap Chela had sold me, I was just sudsing my shirt on my nature-made washboard when the Cora upriver stood up. He was a portly gentleman, not young, and stark naked.

I lost my shirt.

It floated off the rock and down the river on the gentle current.

The next day, two of Chela's nieces, both named Luz, took me to a nicer place to bathe, a gentler place, almost a pool. It did have one drawback: the prevalence of gnats that stung.

"Are there other inhabitants here?" I asked Arcelia's Luz.

"Only leeches," she replied comfortably.

Chela persuaded her sister Arcelia to wash my clothes for me. She took them down to the river every second day.

Chela and Arcelia did not look like sisters. In place of Chela's somewhat overblown features, Arcelia had a rather patrician face, slender, delicate, with a fine, almost aquiline, nose. Her figure was svelte, and she swaggered a little as she started off for the river with my clothes in a pink plastic washtub balanced on top of her head. As soon as she took over my washing, I stopped itching from the detergent and itched only from the bites.

5

On the Brink of Disaster

I had been living in Chela's little house for a couple of months before the government got edgy about me. Don Paco broke the news.
We were eating breakfast in Chela's kitchen.

Don Paco was a big man, going a little thick around the middle
and thin on the crown but still quite handsome. His eyes were very
blue, and his small triangular moustache very Mexican. In those
days, he talked to me in a kind of pidgin Spanish, without articles or
adjectives, only with nouns and verbs.

"Go Presidencia," he said. "Talk Presidente."

Chela was bustling back and forth from the native stove to the
table (she never sat down while Don Paco was eating), but she
stopped bustling as soon as he spoke.

"I saw Flores on the street this morning," he told her in perfectly
understandable Spanish. "He said, 'What's that woman doing in your
house, anyway? What's her game?'"

I was genuinely alarmed. Arnulfo Flores was the Presidente Municipal, the elected chief executive of the Mexican government for the
whole big Cora zone. He was an educated Cora, tough and cheerful.
Even though I did not carry a notebook with me or ask impertinent
questions, Don Arnulfo might easily have taken it into his head that I
was an anthropologist. Very few foreigners of other persuasions
drifted into Jesús María. Anthropologists were not popular in Jesús
María. Don Arnulfo had the power to toughly and cheerfully run me
out of town. And, in spite of the heat and the bugs, I wanted to stay. It

isn't every day that a person past retirement age gets a chance to take care of the sick and hurt and see them get well.

When Don Paco gave me the summons, I had really settled quite comfortably into my little house, too. I still hadn't learned to handle my kerosene stove so it didn't smoke, but, now that I wasn't washing my own clothes, I was finding it very easy to get along with my four buckets of water a day–and I had successfully taken care of the things I decided I didn't need to get used to, the mosquitoes and the cot.

Chela introduced me to Marciano, the young man who made the coffins. With a little tutelage and with screening I brought from Tepic, he made two screened doors for me and a screen for the window. That took care of the flies, June bugs, mosquitoes, and other winged intruders.

He also made me two low sawhorses, and Chela ordered a mat for me like the one the Cora Felipe slept on up on San Miguel. It was made of *otate*, the Mexican bamboo, and stretched from one sawhorse to the other with a short extension at each end. It made a reasonably comfortable bed and one that did not spill me off unless I forgot and sat on the end of it.

I made one other important improvement. I bought yards and yards of cheesecloth in Guadalajara. Chela's sister Arcelia sewed it into two big squares to make "ceilings" for my rooms, to catch any scorpions that might otherwise fall on me.

I was really settling in.

I always ate breakfast in Chela's kitchen after I left the curato. Padre Domingo recommended it because Chela boiled her drinking water. He himself drank out of the river alongside his mule, but he knew that I, being a gringa, was persnickety. I tried not to be, but in Chela's kitchen I was, at the first, apprehensive.

Chela was the most sophisticated mestiza in Jesús María. She had studied nursing in Tepic (although not the final year; it was obstetrics, and her father would not permit her to take it; he was very fastidious, she said). She had visited San Diego. She had performed in the Olympics in Mexico City with a troupe of girls from Tepic to whom she had taught the Cora dances. Unlike most of the women in Jesús María, she could read easily and write pretty well. She could multiply in her head faster than I could on my pocket calculator.

All the same, she had a mud stove in her kitchen, and it had no chimney. The reed ceiling above the stove was black from the smoke.

The stove had two holes in it over the wood fire and a broad flat surface that served as a table for whichever of her nieces or nephews drifted in for a meal. There was room, too, for the stone *metate* on which Chela rolled out the dough for the tortillas.

The kitchen had no window and no screen for the door. It could be infernally hot, and the flies were a pestilence.

It had no sink, either. Sometimes Chela sent the dishes down to the river to be washed by one of her nieces. When she washed them herself, she scrubbed them with a snarl of fibers from a hemp rope and then threw water on them from one pan to the other in a cement trough in the corner of the kitchen. The used water she then flung out into the patio to settle the dust. It was wise not to pass too close to the kitchen door when Chela was washing dishes.

The kitchen usually smelled lovely in the morning, though, for Chela started her fire with *ocote*, the torch pine that makes a smoke as sweet and spicy as incense. Later in the day, the kitchen always smelled cozily of boiling beans.

In the curato, I had learned that it was possible to survive without what nutritionists would label "minimum daily requirements" of anything. I still remember one meal that started with lentils, continued with garbanzos, and ended with beans. There were always plenty of tortillas, though, the meat and potatoes of the poor in Mexico.

With Chela, the usual breakfast was beans with tortillas, and coffee, and even an egg if some of her hens were obliging.

Dinner, when I didn't eat with the bishop, was usually tortillas with pasta, and beans, and something cold to drink—rice water, melon water, sometimes even Pepsi flown in from Tepic. Once in a while, though, there were delicious cooked greens, the quelites that grew wild in the cornfields. Sometimes there were mangos in the summertime and even wild plums. In the spring, back in the curato, we had had *pitahayas*, the vanilla-flavored fruit of the beautiful tall tree cactus.

Once in a long time, there was even meat.

One hot afternoon, a cattleman unknown to me led a steer into town and tied it, protesting, to the big guamuchil tree up the gravel patch from the atrium. The next morning, it was hanging from a branch, skinned, and Don Paco was holding out one hind foot so the owner could cut at the animal's midsection. That day we had liver, and the next day steak, cooked over the fire until it was gray. Don Paco cut the remaining meat into thin, thin strips to hang on the clothesline to dry. Chela salted them and squeezed lemon juice on them to keep off the flies.

On special occasions, Chela would kill a hen and boil it. Once she tried to kill a fryer but couldn't manage it.

"It looked at me and said, '*Peeyu! Peeyu!*'" she said. "'Please don't kill me. I'm too young to die!'"

The hens she did kill were by no means young and were always tough. One hen past laying would serve for Don Paco, and Chela, and me, and two or three nieces and nephews. The broth was always delicious, however, and with tortillas broken into it made quite a filling dish. I had already learned that in the Sierra one does not eat for nutrition but to feel full.

I paid my rent to Chela. The house and the store were hers. She had inherited them from her father, and, here in the Sierra, at least, what a woman has when she marries she has for the rest of her life.

She keeps her maiden name, too. Inez, Juana, Arcelia, and Chela were always known as the Perez sisters, daughters of their father, never by the surnames of their husbands.

I teased Chela.

"In the United States, your name would be different," I told her. "Your name would be Mrs. Joseph Ramirez so everyone would know you were married to Don Paco."

Chela thought for a moment, frowning. Then she exploded. "My name," she said angrily, "is Graciela Perez."

Chela's independence did not in any way diminish Don Paco. On his mule, he was a noble figure, his big sombrero shading his face, his right hand with the reins held high, his left hand on his hip. Helping Chela behind the makeshift counter in the narrow little store with the huaraches hanging at eye level over the crowded aisle, he was affable and impressive. Moreover, he had plenty of cattle of his own on the rancho, high up in the mountains.

There was no doubt about who was head of the house. Chela explained it to me.

"A woman must first obey her father," she told me. "Then her brothers. Then her husband. It is the law of God."

At the look on my face she burst out laughing.

"Oh, you Americans," she said. "You are so funny."

When Don Paco gave me the summons from the Presidente Municipal, however, Chela was not laughing. Neither was I. I was scared, and I think she was, too.

I had to wait until nearly noon to obey the Presidente's command, there were so many sick babies in the curato. Then I walked anxiously through the midday heat. The Coras were inhospitable to outsiders to whom they took a dislike. I did not know Don Arnulfo personally, but his reputation was formidable. I hoped he would not take a dislike to me.

On my way to the Presidencia, I rehearsed what I would say to him. I am an American woman, I would say to him, who worked for many years in New York City. I had a distinguished husband and brilliant children, and I loved them all very much. But my children grew up, my husband died, and I retired. That's when I came to live in Mexico. I have a house just outside of Guadalajara, and I like it there, but I like it here even better. I thought I would tell him how, when I was working in New York, with its gray buildings, its gray pavements, its gray sky, and its gray people, I would long for a place where the sky was blue, the colors bright, and the people kind and uncomplicated.

That was as far as I got when I reached the Presidencia.

The Presidencia was an ancient, disreputable building made of raw adobe. Its plaster and paint were pitted and dirty. Up a short flight of steps, there was a kind of front porch with arches. A few Coras were usually loitering there. Today there were seven. I recognized some of them. I had probably seen all of them before in Chela's store, in Padre Domingo's clinic, or padding down the aisle during Mass with their offerings of cotton disks or nosegays of flowers. None of them spoke to me. All of them eyed me stolidly as I entered the big room inside the Presidencia.

It was almost cool in there, for the ceiling was high and the adobe walls were thick, but it was very dark, as the room had no windows. It seemed to be almost empty, both of furniture and occupants. It took me a minute to find Don Arnulfo. He was a square man, solid, with a good Cora face, very dark and strongly sculptured. He was sitting at a table just inside the door.

I had no chance to make my speech. Without salutation, he went straight to the point.

Why was I here, he wanted to know.

"We Coras are very protective of the costumbre," he said. "The tribal authorities want to know why you are here."

I remembered the Coras who had leaned their elbows on my windowsill.

"When you stayed at the curato with the bishop, we assumed that you were here to help the padres, but now you have a house of your own. Who are you and where are your papers?"

I almost ran back to my little house to fetch the Mexican booklet that certifies that I am a resident alien with permission to live in Mexico legally. Don Arnulfo examined it in a strict, businesslike way. At one point, he looked up at me and said, "No religion."

A number of Coras had drifted in, those from the porch and others. Don Arnulfo and I were surrounded by big white hats and colored shirts, their reds, purples, blues, and greens now softened in the darkness of the room.

"No religion?" I asked stupidly. Don Arnulfo held the book up so I could see. The space after "religion" was blank.

"Nobody asked me," I said.

The Coras who had drifted in all thought that was funny. Happily for me they were laughing now.

The Presidente took back my booklet and read on. When he saw that I was retired—"jubilada," the Mexicans say—he appeared relieved.

He handed me my booklet, rose from his chair, shook my hand, and gave me the courteous Mexican dismissal: "We are at your service."

I walked home under the savage sun, oblivious to the heat, congratulating myself.

In Chela's little house, I told myself, I had proved that I could live without luxuries, without comforts, almost without necessities. In

Padre Domingo's crude little clinic, I had found a place where an old party like me could be of some use. And in this indigenous society, I, an exotic, had been officially accepted.

As I sloped in through the door of my little house, I stubbed my toe on the doorsill and bumped my head hard on the frame.

6

In the Dark of Night

*I*n the curato, I had slept in a room opening onto a quiet patio. As
soon as I began living with a window onto the street, I learned
how much happened at night. Cocks crowed at night. Babies got born
at night. Burros sobbed at night. So I was not greatly surprised when,
at two o'clock in the morning, three men came scratching on my
screen. I was sleeping on the bamboo mat. I had my bed right under
my only window. I sat up.

"Señora, pardon us."

One man spoke for all.

"We come from San Francisco."

San Francisco was a small settlement somewhere up the river. I
had never been there, but I knew more or less where it was.

"We would like to ask you the favor of giving us medicine. A
friend of ours in La Guerra is in terrible pain."

La Guerra. It was still farther up the river, wasn't it?

"*Con todo gusto,*" I lied automatically. "With great pleasure."

I dragged myself out of bed and scuttled into the other room, the
one with a door and no window. My flashlight was useless. The batteries had petered out, and there were no more to be bought in Jesús
María. There was a candle, though, on the floor near the door, with
matches beside it.

It would have been quickest to pull on some slacks and a shirt
over my nightgown, but, for the bishop's sake, I had abandoned
pants. I yanked on some underthings, struggled into a dress, and tied
my shoes on over my bare feet.

"*Vamanos*," I said. "Let's go." I stumbled over the doorsill out onto The Street of San Miguel.

Although the dry season should have started, the rains had not yet stopped. The sky was clouded over and the night so dark I could not see the faces of my three companions. It occurred to me, irrelevantly, that I would probably not go out into the night with three strange men if I were still living on Long Island.

In the atrium of the church, the men's three mules were waiting. I could hear the creak of their saddles as they shifted their weight, but I could barely see them. They were only darker smudges in the darkness of the night.

One of the men had matches with him. He struck one so I could see the keyhole into the burros' entrance to the patio and then another for the keyhole into the big, dark room where the padre kept the medicines. I fumbled for the kerosene lamp.

"Permit me," the man said, as he struck another match and lifted the chimney.

I picked my way with the lighted lamp through the long patio to the door of Padre Domingo's room. He answered my call with a light, wide-awake voice.

"Tell them to saddle my mule," he said.

I helped pack up the medicine and then stood in the atrium and listened as the four mules clattered up the cobbled street to the deep ford up the river. It was starting to rain. I had heard about the trail to La Guerra. In the daytime, they said, it was treacherous. At night, it could be murder. I was suddenly afraid.

The next morning, I had little time to worry about Padre Domingo. It was one of my days to give Doña Emilia one of her final tuberculosis shots. Now that I was handy with the hypodermic syringe, Don Serafim had given me the chore.

Doña Emilia was a frail little old lady who lived with her crippled sister in a one-room adobe house on the hill upriver. I trudged up with my cotton, and alcohol, and syringe, and streptomycin, but her sister told me that Doña Emilia was down at the river washing clothes.

How she got down to the river and back again amazed me, as the trail was very steep and paved with rolling stones, but I figured that if she could do it, I could, too.

Slipping and sliding, I made it down to the flats without disgracing myself and found Doña Emilia just coming out of the river, her wet clothes clinging to her small, thin frame, her clean laundry in a pink plastic pail. I took the pail from her and scolded her as she changed into dry clothes hanging from a bush, changing in that modest way the mestizas had, covered all the time.

I, meanwhile, prepared the shot, and she gave me her beautiful gap–toothed smile as she spread herself over a convenient rock.

We went up the trail together, she in front, as I didn't want her to see how awkward I was, and I in back, to admire the precision with which she placed her worn huaraches on the safe spots in the trail. I left her and the pail at the road and headed for the curato.

She called after me as she always did, "May God accompany you."

When I got back to the curato, there were five Coras sitting on the long hewn log that served as a bench along the front of the church. All wore white muslin pants. All wore big white hats that shaded their humorous faces. Only their shirts were different: five pure, vivid colors.

The one in the violet shirt peeled himself off the bench and sauntered over to me as I opened the burros' entrance with my key. Another rose, stretched, and followed. The real day was beginning.

I took care of those I could easily handle. Those who needed professional help, I led, protesting, to the health center until dinnertime. After dinner, the then doctor would lie in his hammock, saying it wasn't office hours. After dinner, I was on my own.

Padre Domingo plodded in on his dun–colored mule just as I had bandaged the last toe and was closing the burros' door. I opened it again to let him dismount in the patio. A couple of little boys had followed him into the atrium. The hugs he gave them were perfunctory. He was obviously tired.

"The man was really sick," he said. "He's better now."

"Who was it?" I asked.

"A man named Manuel Díaz," he said. "You don't know him."

But I did know him. He and I had sat together by the airstrip at El Cerro, waiting for the plane to come in. He was a wonderful old man. He could set bones and deliver babies, and what he knew he had learned out of books. That, itself, was a miracle here in the Sierra, where so many of the adults sign their names with their thumbs. Don Manuel had taught himself to read.

"What was the matter with him?" I asked.

"An intestinal obstruction," the padre said, as he slid the saddle back to free the mule's tail.

"But he's better now." He said it again.

I didn't ask Padre Domingo how he had cured Don Manuel. I wasn't sure I wanted to know.

"I'm going back to La Guerra in a couple of days," the padre said as he led his mule back to the corral behind the kitchen. "Would you like to go, too?"

Would I like to go! For weeks I had been hoping for a chance to go with Padre Domingo beyond the places I could walk to. Besides, I was eager to see the old man again.

I wasn't sure exactly where La Guerra was, but I found out two days later.

Padre Domingo mounted me on the bishop's outsize mule. It was broad of beam and made broader by the bishop's massive saddle. The padre mounted his own ugly little mule, and two ten-year-old Cora boys walked behind us as we started off.

Chuy watched us from the burros' door, looking worried. The mestiza girls had disappeared from the curato some days ago, and Chuy was now in command. Three other Cora girls came in from their homes to help her every day, and a couple of them slipped out to watch with her as we pattered on our mules out of the atrium.

It was a glorious morning. The rain of the night before had washed the whole world clean. The sky was as blue as a flag, with puffs of clouds to promise more rain later. The mountains were green, and blue, and purple, and unbelievably beautiful.

When we came to the ford in the river, Padre Domingo pulled his left foot out of the stirrup and let one of the Cora boys mount behind him. I copied the padre, and the other boy threw his leg over the mule behind my saddle.

We crossed with our feet tucked up to keep them dry. The water was deep and brown, with an invisible bottom of big, smooth stones.

It smelled of mud. The mules picked their way delicately, heads down, trying to see. On the far side of the river, we stopped to let the boys slide down, and then we started up the trail.

It was as I had heard it described, full of pits and boulders and crumbling along the edges of precipices. There was one place where the padre ordered me to dismount and even did so himself. It was a chute of slick, chalk–white rock, so steep it was almost perpendicular and with only occasional sloping footholds to slide off of. The padre told me that once a brave mestizo had tried to scale it in the saddle and had fallen from the top to the bottom with his mule, dying for valor.

I ascended, trying to brace myself with my hands on the sides of the chute, and twice slipped down to my knees. The two boys walked up as if on the flat, leading the mules after them. I had already ob–served that an Indian almost never falls down.

The bishop's saddle was majestic but monstrous, and the stirrups were inches too short. As the sun rose higher, steam began to rise from the rain–drenched earth. There was no shade, only an occasional thorn tree. There were patches of flowers, however: wild red zinnias, deep–blue morning glories. I hoped that later I would remember the flowers and forget the screaming jockey muscles and the sweat.

The trip seemed interminable but actually lasted only a little over two hours. We pulled up at Don Manuel's house before noon.

The house was in a clearing overlooking the river, a sturdy adobe house with a thatched roof and a good brick floor. Houses, I should say, for there were two: one for cooking, one for sleeping. The clearing was swept clean.

Don Manuel and his wife came out to greet us, Don Manuel still shaky. His gray hair was all ashambles, and he was wearing a wrinkled shirt over a pair of underpants, but his face was seamed with smiles.

We dismounted, I staggering a little from the saddle. The boys took care of the mules, and Don Manuel and his wife and I followed Padre Domingo into the sleeping house. It was immaculate.

Don Manuel and Padre Domingo sat down on the native bed, the frame of wood laced with leather thongs. Don Manuel talked about his illness: how his three friends had come up the river from San Francisco hearing that he was ill; how they had set off for Jesús María at midnight; how he and his wife had then prayed that the padre would come and how he had indeed come, at four o'clock in the morning; how the padre had massaged, and given shots and medicine, and prayed; and how, finally, the padre had cured him.

Women, speckled black rebozos over their heads, came and kept coming until the room was full. There was a narrow table against the wall. Above it stretched a big silk handkerchief with a picture of the Virgin of Guadalupe printed on it. The tablecloth was embroidered with yellow strawberries and edged with a deep border of white crocheted lace with a pattern of prancing horses. On this improvised altar were a wooden cross and one tall candle in a Coca-Cola bottle.

The padre fought his way into some rumpled white ecclesiastical vestments and produced what looked like a medicine bottle with the wine in it and a purse containing the wafers, the Host. He called for a glass of water and celebrated Mass. Don Manuel cried, and everybody else was happy, too.

We ate in the cooking house—Padre Domingo, Don Manuel, the two Cora boys, and I. Don Manuel's wife stood at the native stove, patting and flipping tortillas, good corn tortillas, which we ate moist and hot from the clay griddle. There were *nopales,* the edible cactus, mixed with beans to wrap in a tortilla. There were thin slices of watermelon to eat with our fingers.

It was late in the afternoon when we finally headed for home. The bishop's saddle seemed to have swollen. It seemed to be wider, and the stirrups seemed to be shorter. My legs ached. My knees hurt. All I wanted was to get off and lie down. Even the bishop's mule showed signs of fatigue. Twice she stumbled scrambling up one of the craggy staircases of tumbled rock.

The sun sank behind the mountains to the west, gently rouging the undersides of the cottony clouds gathering above. By the time we reached the chute, the sky had softened to a deep, gentle blue, and the mountains had purpled over. Only the feathery mesquite trees high on a ridge and still in the sun glowed with a light, bright, incandescent green.

I clumsily dismounted. One of the Cora boys led my mule down the chimney, sliding most of the way. I clutched at the sides of the chute as I, too, skidded down the slick, chalky slide.

From the bottom, I could just see Jesús María on the far side of the river. The church still showed white against the smudge of little adobe houses. From here on, I realized gratefully, it wasn't so very far.

It struck me, as I climbed up again on the bishop's outsize mule, that I had another reason to be grateful. It wasn't everybody who had the luck to live in a place where men would go out in the dark of night over a trail like this, looking for help for a friend.

7

Mexico Upside Down

*I*t occurred to me one day, with a sudden flash of delayed insight, that there was something funny about Jesús María. I don't know why I hadn't noticed it before. I had simply taken it for granted and enjoyed it as it was. I tackled Chela.

For once, she was sitting at the dinner table while one of her nieces flipped the tortillas on the flat mud stove–Arcelia's daughter Luz, the tall one with the Scottish surname and the greenish eyes.

The occasion was that Chela had an important guest, an aging uncle from "El Norte," The North. His mother and father had fled to the States with him before Chela was born. They had been loyal supporters of President Francisco Madero, and, with his assassination in 1913, the succession of the drunken President Victoriano Huerta, and the violence right here in the Sierra, they had taken flight, opting for a more peaceful, lawful land. Chela's uncle was visiting Mexico for the first time since his dramatic exit from it so many years ago.

We were all eating together–Chela, Don Paco, Chela's uncle, and I.

"I don't understand this place at all," I said. "Indians in Mexico are supposed to be underdogs. Here in Jesús María, they run everything. They run the government. Don Arnulfo could have thrown me out of town if he had wanted to. They run the school. The only mestizo teachers in Jesús María are those cute girls who are doing their year of social service, those girls from Tepic. The Coras act as if they own the church, too. When I tried to take a picture of that big Christ inside the door, a Cora almost knocked the camera out of my hand. I really wanted that picture, too. Christ had a little bouquet of flowers between his ankles. And the Coras own the land here, don't they? How? Do they have title to it? Is it communal land? I'm confused."

I was really addressing my questions to Chela, but Don Paco answered me. He had discovered that I could follow country Spanish pretty well, so he no longer spoke to me in pidgin. He was looking exceptionally handsome today in a white *guayabera*, the embroidered dress shirt of the elegant Mexican.

"Here the Indians are not pushed off by themselves," he told me earnestly. "Here we all live together." He knitted together the fingers of his two hands to make sure I understood.

It was not precisely an answer. Moreover, it did not seem to me to be precisely true. Chela did not invite Indians into her house and was clearly uncomfortable when I invited them into mine. I did not question Don Paco, as it is not good manners for a woman to dispute a Mexican man, but I did turn to Chela for an answer to my question.

"We and the Coras can't get along without each other," she said comfortably. "The Coras grow corn. We can't get along without corn."

The handmill attached to the stump in the far corner of the kitchen gave silent testimony to that. The preparation of the corn for tortillas was a daily ritual. First, the dry shelled corn was brought to a boil in a little pail full of water that had some lime in it to soften the shells of the kernels. Then it was washed and, handful by handful, ground in the mill. The grinding was hard work. I had tried it and knew. After the corn was ground in the mill, it was ground again on the stone metate, the mortar, and then patted into tortillas to flip on the hot *comal*, or griddle, as Luz was doing now. A hungry man could eat seven or eight tortillas at a meal.

"We can't live without corn," Chela said, "and they can't live without money. We buy their corn, and that gives them money to buy what they need from us."

It certainly was a classic case of taking in each other's washing, but it still didn't explain why the Coras ran the whole show. Chela sensed my bafflement.

"We mestizos haven't been here very long," she said. "Didn't you know?"

I had known, of course, that there had been only Indians in the mountains when the Jesuits persuaded them to come down from their ranchos to build a church and houses here by the river. It had never occurred to me to wonder when the mestizos showed up.

"It was in the revolution," Chela said, "the Cristiada. The Cristeros didn't get here to Jesús María."

I was baffled. I had read about the Cristeros. They were the rebels who rose up against the government when the soldiers were using churches as granaries. It was a bloody time. But what did the Cristeros have to do with Jesús María?

"They weren't the real Cristeros," Chela's uncle took over. "It was after the real Cristeros laid down their arms. The fellows who pretended to be Cristeros, who gave themselves that name, they were nothing but brigands. '*Bragados*,' the people called them. They came right through the Sierra, robbing, and killing, and burning. I was just a little boy, but I remember."

Chela's uncle was a thin, clerkish kind of man in a city suit, dark, of something that looked like rayon. He was wearing a shirt from El Norte with a tie and a tiepin, elegance unheard of in the Sierra. His father had been a judge, he said, and his godfather governor of the state.

"The bragados would come to a house," Chela's uncle said. "They would pound on the door and say, 'What is the sin in this house?' There would be no sin. We were all good Catholics, but the bragados would steal, and kill, and burn the house down just the same."

"But not in Jesús María?" I asked.

"No, not in Jesús María. Maybe they were afraid of the Coras. They say the name Cora means invincible. Maybe they were afraid to come to Jesús María. Maybe there wasn't enough to steal in Jesús María. But in all the other little towns throughout the Sierra where we mestizos lived, they rode in, stole, and burned—and killed, too."

"My father and mother lived in San Juan Peyotan," Chela said. "My father was rich. He had lots of cattle, and goats, and mules, and horses. He had a grove of avocado trees, too. When he and my grandfather knew the Cristeros were coming, they got ready. They went out at night on dark horses, in black hats and black blankets, with black cloths over their mouths and noses. They took all their money and guns and buried them in a well-marked place they could never find again." Chela laughed.

"They say the Sierra is full of treasure," Don Paco said. Don Paco was not of the Sierra. He had met Chela when she was dancing in the Olympics in Mexico City. "But you have to know where to dig."

"When the Cristeros got really near," Chela went on, "my mother and father fled like everybody else. They took the baby, that's my sister Inez, and one saucepan, and the metate, and two bowls. A mule, too. They fled up into the mountains with the Huichols."

"The brigands burned the house," Chela's uncle said. He refused to say Cristeros. "They stole everything. They did the same with almost all the houses in San Juan Peyotan."

"That's why the first mestizo families here came from San Juan Peyotan," Chela said. "They lost everything. They had to run away or be killed."

"So your father and mother didn't come straight here?" I asked.

"Oh, no. The Huichols took care of them until after my sister Juana was born." She laughed. "We always say that Juana is a Huichol, because she was born with the Huichols."

"And then your father and mother came here to Jesús María?"

"No," Chela said. "They went from the Huichols to the Coras, to a rancho up on the other side from here. The Coras took care of them up there."

"But, then, when did your parents come down here?" I asked, bewildered.

"Before Arcelia was born. The Cora governor said that they would be safe down here and that they could come. He wanted my father to start a store. We were the very first mestizo family in Jesús María."

"So you were born here, too."

"Yes. I was born here, and my mother died when I was two, leaving my father with four little girls. He kept us all and took care of us," Chela said proudly.

"But he had to give up the store. He couldn't take the burros and go to Ruiz anymore to buy sugar, and coffee, and salt, and things like that. He couldn't leave us alone. It's a long way to Ruiz. It took him days to go and come back."

Chela had put on her smart multicolored print in honor of her uncle, the dress she had bought at great price the last time she went to Puerto Vallarta.

"My father was so poor without the store," Chela went on, "that we lived in a *kareton*."

A kareton is a bamboo room on stilts. To get into it, you climb up a notched log.

"But we couldn't sleep in the kareton," Chela said. "My father would go off to work at four o'clock in the morning, and he'd leave us on the big native bed out in the open, where the scorpions couldn't fall on us from the roof. We'd lie there looking up at the stars, saying, 'Come home, Papa. Come home.' Then, when he did come home, we'd all have to get out of bed and kneel down on the ground while he prayed a Rosary."

"And the governor who invited your father to come down here, was he of the Mexican government or the tribe?"

"The tribal government," Chela said. "We didn't have any Mexican government then. Not until I was six or seven. Then we got a Presidente Municipal. He was elected for a year, but he got killed in San Francisco soon after he took office. Everybody was very angry about that, I remember. There's even a song about it."

"Was he a mestizo?"

"No, no." Chela laughed. "The officials here are always Coras."

"Because the land belongs to the Coras?"

Chela evaded the question.

"The Coras are educated," she said. "We're not. The Coras had the institute. We only had the rural primary school, first, second, and third grades. We were lucky. There were only three other rural schools in the whole Sierra. People my age who came here from other towns have to ask their children to read to them. My sisters and I can read and write pretty well, because my father insisted that we keep going to school. So my sisters and I went to the third grade year after year after year." She laughed again.

"What on earth was the Instituto?" I asked.

"It was in the days of Cardenas," Chela's uncle said.

"It was a school for Indians," Chela said. "All the important Indians went to it. A lot of them have important government jobs in other places now, but Arnulfo Flores and a few others are still here. It was a boarding school, full of Indians."

"It was in the days of Cardenas," Chela's uncle said again. "He wanted to Mexicanize the Indians."

Arnulfo Flores. He who had given me permission to stay in Jesús María. Would he be willing to tell me about the Instituto or would he think I was prying? I decided to try my luck and called on him the following afternoon.

He was sitting on a native stool under the mesquite tree in the patio of his very solid house, a house obviously of adobe but plastered and cleanly painted white. His wife, Doña Constancia, was sitting on the ground, her hand loom attached to the tree. She was weaving a bag with a pattern of deep grayish yellow on a white cotton background. It was going to be a very handsome bag.

The two of them greeted me cordially, and Don Arnulfo went into the house to get me a chair. We chatted amiably about the tranquility of Jesús María, about Don Arnulfo's tough enforcement of his own law against the sale of beer and hard liquor. "Just a little for the fiestas, of course," he said. We discussed the rumor of the murder of a mestizo in one of the mestizo towns a couple of days away, and then I asked him about the Instituto.

"It was in the days of President Cardenas," Don Arnulfo said. "He wanted to educate us, to make Mexicans of us." Just as Chela's uncle had said.

"I was thirteen when the soldiers came for me. I lived away up in the mountains. The soldiers came with guns. They picked up one hundred of us, fifty boys and fifty girls, mostly Coras but some Huichols, too. If our fathers objected, the soldiers tied them up and brought them down here and threw them in jail.

"There inside the school they made us take off our clothes and put on uniforms, blue. Then they made a pile of our own clothes and burned them while we stood in a circle around the fire, crying."

Don Arnulfo stayed in the Instituto four years, he told me, through the second grade. He could read but had no idea what the words meant because he really didn't know Spanish. From Jesús María , the government sent him to another school for Indians in the state of Hidalgo, then on to another near Tepic.

"We just had a cup of gruel and one bun for breakfast, and four tortillas and a cup of rice for dinner," he said. "I was hungry all the time. The other boys took jobs with carpenters, but I worked for a baker so I could eat bread." He laughed.

Then he came back to Jesús María, and the government sent him to teach school in one little mountain settlement after another.

"But I still didn't know anything," Don Arnulfo said cheerfully, "so I went back to Tepic to normal school. Constancia went with me. We had a baby then."

Doña Constancia looked up from her loom and smiled at me.

"We were very poor. We just had one room, but we had a little stove. Constancia cooked beans on the stove, and our friends gave us tortillas. We stayed there until I graduated."

"And the Instituto?" I asked.

"It closed after Cardenas," Don Arnulfo said. "Then Don Serafim had half of the building for a clinic, and they had the rural school in the other half. That was for Coras and mestizos, too."

"That wasn't the school we went to," Arcelia, Chela's sister, told me later. "The institute was still full of Coras when we went to school."

"But where *was* the institute?" I asked Arcelia. She and her three children were living in two rooms at the end of Chela's patio, behind the tree where the hens roosted at night. Her own house had melted down in the August rain.

"Where the new school is now," she said. "They tore down the old building to put up the new school. Don Arnulfo used to be principal of it, but now he's just head of the Board of Education and Presidente Municipal."

That seemed to me to be about enough for one man, even a man like Don Arnulfo.

"But the Coras kept on getting educated," Arcelia said. "One of Don Arnulfo's sons is a teacher, and there are lots of others."

"What was it like here when you were little?" I asked Arcelia.

"Oh, it was wonderful," she said. "There were very few houses here then. The Coras mostly lived on their ranchos and only came down here for the fiestas. They didn't speak any Spanish. We had to learn to speak Cora. They loved my father, though. When he died, they came in from all over the Sierra and cried and cried.

"He would never wear store clothes. He always wore a shirt of white unbleached muslin and white muslin pants, like the Coras. Only the Coras didn't wear pants," she said, "when we were little."

"When did they start?" I asked.

"With the Instituto," she said. "The Instituto changed a lot of things. We had soldiers here then."

"You say there were very few houses," I said. "What about the mestizos? Didn't they all come to escape the bragados? Didn't they all have houses?"

"Oh, no," she said. "Only three families of us stayed. Some came and went back home when the danger was past. Many mestizo families who live here now haven't been here long at all. They just came because Jesús María is the city of the Sierra."

She thought a minute.

"Of course, there are more Coras living here now," she said, "because their children are in school."

She laughed again.

"But when we were little, it was wonderful. We were very poor. Sometimes we only had two dresses each, one to put on and one to wash in the river. But we were happy. Happy."

"But you were completely isolated here, weren't you?"

"Oh, no," Arcelia said. "We had a postman, Don Arnulfo's uncle. He went to Tepic every two weeks with a bag of mail, five days in and five days back."

"On a mule?"

"No, on foot. It would have taken twice as long on a mule."

"When did he stop going?"

"When they made the airstrip up on El Cerro, after Don Serafim and before the padres. Then we could send messages back and forth on the plane."

And the church? Don Arnulfo mentioned it. He said that when he was little, sometimes a priest would come in a long tattered black habit, barefoot, to marry and baptize. But he himself knew nothing, Don Arnulfo said, not even how to bless himself. The older Coras knew, but not those like him who had gone away to school. He didn't know anything, he said, until the Americans came.

"Americans?" I asked Chela later.

"They were here during your world war," she said. "They were missionaries back from China or one of those places. They built that room where the padre keeps the medicines."

They should see it now, I thought, before it falls down.

"I kept house for them. They taught how to cut a cross where a scorpion stings and suck out the poison. They couldn't speak Spanish very well, but they were lovely men. After the war they went away again, back to China or someplace like that, I guess."

"And then the Franciscans came?"

"Oh, that was much later. The Franciscans have only been here a very few years. Everything has been different since they came."

I asked the bishop later.

He had seen Jesús María first from the air, he said, flying in to El Cerro. He and a padre had walked down the burro trail to the town.

"The church was a ruin," he said. "It was falling down. It had no windows and was as hot as an oven. The door had no key, only two wooden spikes and a rope to keep it closed. I had to beg the Coras to make every little repair. At first, they gave their permission very reluctantly, and they didn't allow us to touch any of the santitos. But, little by little, we were able to restore the church, open the windows, build back the fallen towers, reinforce the walls, and tile the floor. Finally, when all the repairs had been made, Don Nazario, the tall, elderly Cora who supervises the costumbre in the church, came to see me. We had made the church very pretty, he said. Now could we restore the santitos? Some were in very poor shape, some without hand or arm, one with half its face gone."

The statues in the church were an unbelievable collection–from the sophisticated antiquities the bishop said probably came from Guatemala in the seventeenth century, through touching primitives, to sentimental moderns apparently made of plastic. Every santito had two Cora caretakers, appointed for a year, who respectfully removed such offerings as had worn out their power and who protected their charges from the depredations of tourists with cameras.

The most important santito, the one most beloved of the Coras, was not on view. It was Christ in the tomb, concealed in a casket under the window on the left side of the nave. The bishop had imported an artist to restore them all.

The church, and the santitos, and the big brass candlesticks still belonged to the Coras, and their offerings of cotton disks and nosegays were always there to attest to their religious devotion.

By the time I reached Jesús María, however, the mestizos were treating the church as if it were also their own. Mestiza women often mopped the floor after Cora men had swept it, and twice I accompanied Chela at night to make sure that all the candles were lighted in their little amber tumblers.

With the church had come another kind of interdependence between the Coras and the mestizos, much more personal than that of the corn. Although few of the Coras went to Mass (except for those celebrated especially for them), almost all of them brought their children to the church to be baptized, and the godparents were often mestizos. The relationship of coparenthood thus established placed responsibility on the godparents almost greater than if they had been related by blood, a responsibility that Chela and Don Paco, at least, accepted with grace. Chela was her godmother, Chuy told me, and had given her the little silver cross she always wore on a chain around her neck.

But even without this coparent relationship, the Coras and the mestizos were tolerant of each other. They did not live together in the way that Don Paco's knitted fingers suggested, but they did live with a kind of jocular affection between them. The Coras were top dog and knew it. The mestizos knew it, too, and accepted it philosophically.

As I was saying good–bye in Chela's patio to her uncle, who was leaving for Cleveland, a file of men on mules appeared over the top of the mountain behind us. As they maneuvered the switchback, I could see that one was a Huichol with his hands tied behind his back. The others were all Coras.

"The police," Chela said, "bringing in a prisoner."

"The police are all Coras?" I asked stupidly.

Chela looked at me hopelessly.

"Of course," she said.

All of the men looked inexpressibly weary, but it did not seem incongruous to me that the policeman in the lead, the Cora in the peacock blue shirt, was carrying a bunch of orchids in his hand.

The sight of the prisoner and his captors reminded me that I had never asked anybody about the law and its enforcement. I asked Chela later.

"If it's a big crime," she said, "the police take the prisoner to Tepic, but that doesn't happen very often."

"We Coras don't kill very often," Don Arnulfo had told me. "We just hire a witch."

"If it's only a dispute," Chela continued, "the Cora judge settles it here. Paco saw a little pig that belonged to Filemon in a Cora's corral. Paco knew it was Filemon's because he had given Filemon the pig and had clipped its ear. The judge decided in favor of the Cora but kept the pig himself to cover the court costs. You can't win against a Cora," she said matter-of-factly.

The minority complaint from just about everywhere.

With two communities so different from each other in their backgrounds and beliefs, one could not expect that one group would admire everything about the other. In my first early days in Jesús María, I became aware that the mestizos' attitude toward the Coras was tainted with condescension and that the Coras' attitude toward the mestizos was tinged with scorn.

I reported to Chela a visit I had made to the house of a Cora woman.

"I wouldn't go into a Cora house," Chela advised me. "You might get fleas."

When I was watching the drip from Felipe's I.V. up on the mesa of San Miguel, I told his mother that I would love to have a house up there.

"Come ahead," she said. "Build a house. We'll help you. Nothing bad can happen to you up here. Up here there's nothing but Coras."

She waggled a finger down in the direction of town.

"No mestizos like down there," she said.

The little partition between the two communities displayed itself even in contemplation of the corn on which all their lives depended.

"Don't eat the tortillas the Cora women make," Chela warned me. "They wipe their hands on their aprons."

"The mestizas make terrible tortillas," Chuy contended. "They don't wash the corn properly before they grind it."

The basis on which the whole social structure rested was, of course, very simple. The Coras as a tribe owned the land. The mestizos were tenants. Nothing was going to change that.

The result was tranquility. I could walk alone, at three o'clock in the morning, to the most distant house in Jesús María in perfect safety except, perhaps, from the dogs. The rule of the Coras and the acceptance of the mestizos had their reward in a peaceful, law-abiding town.

Somebody ought to write a book about this place, I told myself. There can't be another like it on the map.

Then I had to correct myself. Jesús María wasn't on the map.

On my map of Mexico, there was a fair-sized blank space in the middle of which Jesús María ought to have been. And wasn't.

8

It's Easy to Get to Tepic

When I told my friends in Guadalajara how far Jesús María was from so-called civilization, they quailed. (I would have quailed, too, when I first came to Mexico.) They were particularly dashed by the lack of communication. "No telephone? No telegraph? But surely you have radio communication!"

We did have a little of that, but the radio was in the Presidencia and communicated only with the Presidencia in Tepic. The one time the people of Jesús María would have liked some outside information (to find out if it was true that a visiting priest burned up when the commercial plane he was flying in ran into the side of a mountain), the battery of the radio was dead. There was no gasoline for the motor to revive the battery until José clattered into town in the Datsun. Gasoline from the pickup truck's tank fed the motor that charged the battery, and questions spewed out over the airwaves—but there was no answer. It was Saturday afternoon, and the Presidencia in Tepic was closed.

The rumor was true. The plane had crashed. The priest had expired, along with the pilot and three other passengers.

Most of the time, however, we did not feel deprived. Living in a place so isolated, one loses the sense that it is remote. It becomes the center of the universe, and it is the rest of the world that is far away.

Every month, however, I had to leave the center of the universe and make my way to far-off Guadalajara. There were those Huichol students in my house there. I had to see how they were faring, if they were healthy, if they were doing well in school, if they were eating properly, if they were winning their soccer games. I took care of them, and they took care of my house, making it possible for me to stay in the Sierra for most of the month.

They were a pleasure to come home to with their good temper, good manners, and their acute appreciation of the funny side of life. In the few days I could be with them, I could read my mail, deposit a check or two, pay my gas and light bills, and even have a word or two of English with some of my compatriots.

I enjoyed my little respites in Guadalajara, and, if all went well, it was easy enough to get there. I simply flew to Tepic, drove four hours over the two-lane mountain road from Tepic to Guadalajara, and eventually arrived home. It was especially easy when I still got a lift in the mission plane, before I decided that a couple of gunnysacks of corn were worth more than I was. Padre Jacinto continued to land on the sandy little airstrip down by the river long after the commercial pilots had prudently opted for the safer airstrip up on top of the mountain, the airstrip up at El Cerro. Now I had to fly from there in the six-seater commercial plane.

It took off twice a week, loaded, and often overloaded, with passengers from settlements down and around the mountain and with the passengers' bulging cartons and sugar sacks, the luggage of the poor in Mexico.

At first, to get to El Cerro we had to slide down the hill from Jesús María and trudge across the flats to the canastilla, lugging along whatever we were taking with us. After being hitched across the river on the canastilla, we would get a lift from José to the mountaintop and the airstrip. Later, however, the Coras carved out a switchback down the cliff on the far side of the river, and the dapper José could maneuver the pickup down to a ford and could splash across the river and sputter up the hill, right to Jesús María. We could then climb into the Datsun right there, without even having to carry our things to the canastilla. We were really traveling Pullman.

Sometimes, of course, the Datsun didn't come. Sometimes it had no gasoline.

José had to depend for gasoline on the commercial pilot, who would open a little spigot in the plane's gasoline tank to drain off some for José. Sometimes the plane had no gasoline to spare.

Sometimes the Datsun developed symptoms. Then it would have to wait for a mechanic flown out from Tepic to cure it.

Sometimes José was not in residence. Sometimes he slipped aboard the plane and escaped for a few days of rest and recreation in Tepic.

If we knew beforehand that the Datsun was not going to show up, Don Gustavo, Juana's husband, would escort me up to the airstrip on one of his gentle mules.

Don Gustavo was a lovely man, homely in a lean, attractive way, always cheerful and often amused. He was amused that I didn't know how to ride a Mexican saddle very well and sometimes forgot and posted to the trot. He was amused when I asked questions about things that any intelligent country person would know without asking. He was kind and patient, and I was conscious of how lucky I was that he was Chela's brother-in-law.

We would start off before dawn, my battered suitcase strapped on behind Don Gustavo's saddle. We would cross the river where José crossed in the Datsun. Then, disdaining the road, we would clatter over the boulders that skirted the river on up to the huge wild fig tree. There we would meet the road as it rumbled down from one mountain to scramble up the next. But, again, we would scorn it. Instead, we would climb up, down, and around the mountains on old trails known to Don Gustavo.

Through the prickly underbrush, past the green tree cactus making long, soft shadows in the early light. Past the black volcanic rocks where ghosts of the Coras were said to gather. Past the silk cotton trees with kapok bursting out of their pods. Past the stands of trees clustered together, mesquite, guamuchil, acacia. On up to Don Basilio's little rancho on top of the mountain, beside the airstrip at El Cerro.

There Don Gustavo would leave me, leading my riderless mule back down the trails to the river, and I would wait for the plane to come in.

El Cerro was the junction of the trails that led up from the settlements on all sides down the mountain. To get from one settlement to another, it was almost always easiest to go by way of El Cerro. It was also the pivot at which we mentally exchanged the gentle mule for the hurtling taxi, the sweet air of the mountains for the sugary smoke of Tepic's sugar mill, Chela's cluttered, dusty little store for the polished aisles of Tepic's haughty branch of a Guadalajara dress shop. It was where one life ended and another began.

Getting up to El Cerro with Don Gustavo was pleasantly adventurous. Getting up there in the pickup truck sometimes presented problems.

There was the day, soon after Don Arnulfo had given me leave to stay in Jesús María, when Don Paco was going to ask José to make a plane reservation for me with Don Basilio, but José had not driven into Jesús María that morning. It was noon before I discovered that Don Basilio had not been told that I wanted to fly into Tepic the following day. Don Basilio, living as he did right beside the airstrip, was the ticket vendor for the plane.

Don Paco told me not to worry, that I didn't need a reservation, that I should have no trouble getting a ticket on arrival at El Cerro in the morning.

I did worry, though. The only other time I had gone up without a reservation, there had been no room for me in the plane. It flew off without me and didn't fly back until four days after my dentist appointment in Guadalajara. I wanted a reservation.

Chela came to my rescue.

"You can ask José yourself," she said soothingly. "He has started coming down to eat dinner here in Jesús María."

I, working in the clinic, hadn't known that before.

"He leaves the Datsun on the far side of the river now," she said. "The horses and mules have trampled the ford so he can't cross."

"Where does he eat?" I asked Chela.

"With Cassiana," she said. "I think."

Cassiana lived in a little stone house on the ledge, half a kilometer upriver from the church. I set out for it in the brutal noonday sun.

"José doesn't eat here anymore," Cassiana told me. "I think he eats with the teacher Alfredo's mother-in-law now."

I trudged home to ask Chela.

"Who is the teacher Alfredo's mother-in-law and where does she live?"

Chela told me, and I set off again. I found José. He was reclining gracefully in the lacy shade of a mesquite tree listening to his radio, which was playing Mexican country music at top volume.

"I want to go to Tepic tomorrow," I shouted at him. "Could you please do me the favor of making a reservation for me with Don Basilio?"

He turned down the radio, and I repeated the question.

"Why not?" he replied politely. "With pleasure."

"And may I please ride up to the airstrip with you?"

"Of course," he said. "I leave from the other side of the river now. The animals have trampled the ford."

"What time?" I asked.

"Seven o'clock sharp," he replied. "The plane has been coming in early."

With appropriate expressions of gratitude, I left and returned to Chela. Now that José was not crossing the river, I would have to make sure about the canastilla.

"Do you know who has the grapple now?" I asked Chela. Men seemed to take turns.

"Victoriano," she said. "I think."

Victoriano lived near the base of the lava flow. His wife came to the door of his little adobe house. With her came the sweet, warm smell of boiling beans.

I told her I was leaving for Tepic in the morning and would need a lift across the river.

"What a pity," Victoriano's wife said. "Victoriano has gone to the rancho and won't be home until day after tomorrow. The teacher Alfredo wants to go, too, but we can't find the grapple anywhere."

I had obviously seen the moon over the wrong shoulder.

Dinner was ready when I got back to Chela's. Don Paco was already eating. Chela was flipping tortillas at the stove. I sat down at the table.

"I'll need a mount tomorrow to cross the river," I said apologetically, and I told them about Victoriano and the grapple. "A burro will do," I said.

"To cross the river?" Chela was incredulous. "Can't you cross yourself? On the bridge?"

"The bridge?"

"The bridge. Just down the river from where the men are digging. Haven't you seen it?"

"You mean those stones?" It was my turn to be incredulous. There did seem to be a row of rocks sticking up above the water below where some men were digging (to sink the foundations for a real bridge, Don Paco had told me).

"Yes," Chela said. "Can't you cross there? The water is quite shallow if you should happen to fall in."

"But I don't want to fall in," I protested. "I don't want to wet my city clothes or ruin my camera or my typewriter."

"Oh," Chela said. "You want an animal for your things."

"Yes," I said. "And for myself. A burro will do."

"Of course," Chela said kindly, still not believing that anyone could be so craven. "Paco will lend you ours."

In the morning there was no burro. Don Paco was asleep and so was Chela. Sadly, I stowed my typewriter and my camera in the storage carton under the bamboo mat I called my bed. Carrying only a light suitcase and my hand-woven Cora bag, I plodded through the town, slid down the hill, and crossed the flats to the river. Half a dozen men with shovels and pickaxes were excavating a big hole. Among them was Don Gustavo, Juana's husband, my friend.

The bridge was, indeed, downriver. The nature of rivers being that where they are shallow they are also wide, the bridge looked to be at least a city block long. It was made of boulders placed so that one could cross dry stepping, and sometimes leaping, from stone to stone. It was a crossing supremely suitable for a goat.

Don Gustavo put down his shovel, left the group of workmen, took my suitcase, and strode on ahead.

I picked my way to the river. Stepping from rock to rock was not as hard as I had thought it would be, until I came to a gap where a tree trunk had been shoved between two stones. I hesitated, trying to figure out which foot to take off on. A strong hand grasped mine. I swiveled my head around and saw a tall, graying man. I knew him as Don Ricardo. He, too, had been working in the excavation.

"I'll help you, Doña Cata," he said. The most beautiful words in the world if one is stuck in the middle of a river.

He left me at the far bank and leapt back over the bridge to start work again.

The trail up the cliff was almost vertical and very skiddy. I slipped and grabbed a spiny sapling. Then there was Don Gustavo again, sliding down the trail, having deposited my suitcase on the road up above. He smiled, grabbed my hand, and hauled me up to level ground. Then he, too, left me and skidded down the cliff to cross the river and get back to his digging.

The end of the road widened out into a kind of circle where the Datsun could turn around. The Datsun, however, was not there. A Cora girl was sitting on the mountain side of the road, nursing her baby. I sat down on a rock beside her.

She was a pretty girl, her dark hair caught back with two plastic combs, one green and one pink. Her purple blouse had a ruffle of lace and was piped with blue. Her gold filigree earrings dangled almost to her shoulders, and attached to one of her strings of beads was a common safety pin. I was sorry my camera was under the bed.

"Have you seen José?" I asked her.

She ducked her head and turned away, clutching her baby closer.

I looked at my watch. It was exactly seven o'clock. The plane just might come in early. Thus had spoken José.

An iridescent black beetle was doggedly pushing a large ball of dung over the pits and ruts of the road. I sat admiring it, willing myself not to look again at my watch. The minutes ticked on.

The girl finished nursing her baby. She pulled down her bodice and turned to me shyly.

"He said he'd come back," she said, so softly I could barely hear her. "José said he'd come back."

"I'm waiting for my husband." She called him her señor. "I have tortillas for him."

I had noticed the hand-woven wool bag at her side. It was obviously full of something.

"He's working on the other side," she confided. "Digging."

It was 7:45 when her señor leapt up over the side of the cliff. He was a lithe, slender youth with a dark, gentle face. His white cotton pants, tied at the ankle, were smudged with mud, and his orange shirt was dirty. He sat down on the other side of the girl, took the baby in his arms, and began talking to it softly in Cora.

The girl pulled tortillas out of her bag and handed them, one at a time, to her young husband. He ate them hungrily, still talking to the baby.

Suddenly, the Datsun roared down and around the side of the mountain. I stood up, but José wagged his finger at me, "No," as he slowed to make the turn toward the switchback. Then he held up a sheaf of papers, pointed across the river, put down the papers, and held up his hand with the thumb and forefinger almost touching. "I'll only be a minute," the familiar gesture promised.

The young Cora gently handed the baby back to its mother and then sprang up to leap into the back of the pickup. I watched as the Datsun disappeared over the brink of the cliff and then appeared below, splashing across the river. In spite of the mules and horses having trampled it, the ford seemed still to be negotiable. The Datsun disappeared into Jesús María, over the brow of the hill.

The girl tied her baby on her back and picked up her bag.

"I'm going now," she said and moved up the perpendicular trail as nimbly as a she-goat.

The sun was almost over the mountain when the Datsun appeared once more. It jittered down the hill and into the river and stopped. Dead. I died a little, too. I had been in Jesús María three weeks. I was ready to go home.

After a short wait, a passenger squirmed out of the right-hand window. I recognized him as Alfredo, the Cora teacher. He snaked out over the fender without getting his feet wet and released the catch so the hood slowly rose. As he squirmed back through his window, José slithered out of his own, a white rag in his hand. The points were dried, and the motor would start.

It was 8:37.

We made it to the airstrip in record time. I was sitting between José and the teacher Alfredo. The sun shone mercilessly into our eyes whenever the nose of the truck pointed east. It was hard to understand how José could possibly see to drive, but drive he did, winding and climbing and skidding around turns in the perilous track, passing the marker that commemorated the first Datsun's rolling down the cliff, and finally, miraculously, reaching Don Basilio's rancho.

The plane had not yet come in.

The little houses in Don Basilio's rancho were quite new and obviously made by hand. There were four of them: a cook house, a sleeping house, a house for storing things, and a kareton. All four had thatched roofs, and the walls of the sleeping house were shaggily thatched as well.

Three saddled mules were tethered outside the cook house. Their owners were inside, breakfasting. Down at the end of the road, three men were squatting on their heels and obviously enjoying a gossip, for I could hear them laughing. I recognized one of them as Don Basilio.

Don Basilio was a jocular, egg-shaped man with a toothbrush moustache and a propensity for coloring every sentence with at least one naughty word. He was hunkered down now with the two other men, and I was sure the laughter was for one of his harmless obscenities.

José spun the Datsun around to head back to the river, and the teacher Alfredo and I ducked into the cook house.

It was made of saplings lashed together and had a dirt floor. There was no door in the narrow opening, only a shaky wooden gate to keep out the pig. Doña Dora, Don Basilio's wife, presided at the mud stove, dishing out beans in their broth and cinnamon tea to all who drifted in to eat. One of her daughters flipped tortillas on the big clay grill.

The three men of the mules were at a bare, wooden table when I followed the teacher in through the door. Two were on a tottery bench on the far side, one on the near bench, also tottery. He slid over so the teacher and I could sit down beside him.

I knew the man on our side. He was a mestizo who had brought me a jarful of worms to show me the success of a medicine I had given his little daughter. The other two were unknown to me. They eyed the teacher Alfredo and me without interest.

Doña Dora served us impassively. She was a slight, sturdy woman with two thin black braids hanging down in front of her shoulders. She had a dark, clever face and regarded us, her customers, with tolerance and her irrepressible husband with mirth.

We ate in silence, the teacher and I because who knew when the plane would come in, the men across the table because it was their custom. The mestizo observed us, smiling a little as he, too, finished his breakfast.

The two men slid off their bench. One of them reached up for a package of cheap cigarettes and one of chewing gum from the open cupboard on the wall behind them. Then they both slapped some money on the table and swaggered out of the gate to mount their mules and ride away.

When the teacher and I had finished with our beans and tortillas, we paid Doña Dora over her protests and strolled out across the gravel yard to seat ourselves in the shade of the sleeping house, along with the mestizo whose daughter had been cured of worms. The sun was now hot and higher in the sky.

I could see the inside of the sleeping house. It had a dirt floor, but the bed in there was from Tepic with a headboard of plastic, heavily ornamented. There was a sewing machine in there, too, a treadle machine, not the kind I had seen in Jesús María, the kind with a wheel you have to turn by hand. Don Basilio and Doña Dora were not poor, Chela had told me. Don Basilio almost always had a job of some kind. He could read and write. He had been in charge of the gang of Coras who had chopped out the road down to the river, and now he made money storing cargo that came in by air until the consignees picked it up. Also, the crates and crates of Pepsi and Coke bottles behind the cook house testified to a brisk business in beverages safer than the available water that came up from the river in oil cans.

The mestizo, the teacher, and I sat in companionable silence, idly watching the life of the rancho. We had no excuse now for apprehension. Sooner or later, the plane would swoop around the prow of the hill, and we would stroll out to the airstrip to board it. I put my woven Cora bag on the ground to rest my shoulder.

A rooster chased a wildly fleeing hen across the yard. The sow rolled luxuriously in the puddle Doña Dora had made for her beside the kareton. A turkey-cock strutted by, spread his tail, and thumped down his wings, looking excessively handsome and silly. Don Basilio sauntered up from the airstrip, waved at us, and ducked into the cook house.

The mestizo broke the silence.

"When are you going to The North, Señora Cata?" he asked me.

When the States were not The Other Side, they were always The North.

"Take me with you. You can say I'm your son."

He grinned at me, showing off his even white teeth under his luxuriant moustache. He was very dark. We did not look related.

"I'm afraid we would have to swim the river," I said. Then I re–membered what he had told me before.

"But you've been in the United States already, haven't you?" I asked him.

"Many times. Many times," he said. "First as a bracero. That was beautiful. I was legal."

He thought for a moment, and then he laughed.

"But you can't sleep on the street up there. If you get tired here, you lie down. Up there, a policeman comes along and pokes you with his toe. 'What's the matter with you?' he says. 'Are you sick? Are you drunk? Where are your papers?' "

"And you haven't any?" I asked, really knowing the answer

"Only when I was a bracero," he said. "Then I was legal. That was beautiful."

"You must have been very young," I said. "That was a long time ago."

"I was young, but I was strong," he said. "Yes, it was a long time ago."

We were silent for a little while, and then he spoke again.

"Well," he said, "if you won't take me with you, bring me a radio, one with a tape recorder in it."

Don Basilio came out of the cook house, his clipboard in his hand.

"And bring me a blonde," he said.

I had heard the joke before, but we all laughed.

"You're late," he told the teacher Alfredo and me. "The others paid on time."

Then he checked us off as we handed over our money.

It was three o'clock when the plane finally swooped in. We had almost given it up, as the pilots did not like to fly over the mountains in the afternoon owing to the turbulence. I picked my Cora bag off the ground, the mestizo carried my suitcase out to the airstrip, and we waited while four passengers spilled out of the plane along with bulging plastic bags, paper cartons, and a stack of men's sombreros piled one on top of another. The mestizo claimed a couple of cartons and said good-bye to us as the teacher and I climbed into the plane with two mestizos who had been patiently sitting by the airstrip all day. One of them had half a dozen Rhode Island Reds with their feet tied together. He held them with their heads hanging down, squawking, six protesting clumps of feathers.

We adjusted ourselves to the bags and boxes piled around us, and to the hens, and settled down for takeoff. The little plane spun around with a great spewing-out of gravel behind it and hummed down the airstrip almost to the end before it lifted itself into the air.

When we touched down in Tepic, it was too late to drive to Guadalajara. Night would fall while I was still in the mountains. Besides, my battery was dead.

After a death-defying dash in a taxi, I fetched up at a friendly motel, ate some dinner, telephoned the Huichol students to tell them I would be home the next day, and started to prepare for the night. I was tired. I emptied the contents of my woven Cora bag onto the bed. A scorpion stalked out, its stinger curled indignantly over its head.

It seemed a fitting ending to what had been, with the exception of a couple of social interludes, a rather trying day.

As I drifted off to sleep that night, lulled by the scream of brakes, the clash of gears, and the smell of toilet deodorant, I remembered what Don Basilio had asked me as I climbed into the plane.

"When are you coming back?" he asked me.

"In eight days," I told him, the Sierra equivalent of a week.

"Then you'll be back in time for the wedding," he whispered. "I'll send the Datsun for you. I'm going to kill a cow."

My last thoughts were of El Cerro. Who was getting married? Where on that rancho would they have the wedding? What would they do with the sow?

9

A Bride Wears Blue

I dressed carefully for the wedding. Not to scandalize the bishop, I put a dress over my slacks, the skirt of it coming to well below my knees. I had learned from some of the modest mestizas how to make an awkward compromise between decorum and common sense. The only women who appeared in slacks in Jesús María were either the rare tourists or the government types, like the social-service girls who came to teach the Cora women how to sew. (The Cora women! They sewed their men's shirts with such tiny stitches, so doubled back, that their stitching looked as if it had been done by machine.)

I was wearing slacks because word had come down the day before that Don Basilio was sending mules for the bishop and me. José had slipped off to Tepic, and there was nobody else to drive the Datsun. It was fine with me. I felt a lot safer on a mule than in the pickup truck with the dashing José at the wheel.

I was aware that Don Basilio's invitation was more for my camera than for me, but I didn't mind. I had never been to a wedding on a rancho before and was glad of a chance to take pictures.

I had no idea who was getting married or to whom. I had thought all of Don Basilio's daughters were married already, but perhaps there was a younger sister or a niece. The bishop was obviously going to celebrate the nuptial Mass and obviously knew whom he was marrying, but I didn't bother to ask.

The mules were scheduled to arrive at 10:30, and I was in Padre Domingo's little clinic then, rubbing an old Cora's knee with a sticky mixture of peyote and alcohol. The bishop was in his room at the far end of the patio typing, as he did every day, on his clattery old office typewriter. Having learned that no Mexican is slave to the clock, I kept on happily working in Padre Domingo's clinic, not worrying about when the mules would appear. Finally, at 11:30, after three sick babies, a burned hand, and a case of dandruff, Don Basilio himself sauntered in through the big worm-eaten doors.

"José came back," he said, smiling.

Then he strolled down the patio while I slipped into the women's bathroom and gratefully divested myself of my slacks, which I hung on a nail in the shower. Then, feeling a great deal less foolish, I hurried out to the Datsun, parked in front of the atrium. José was at the wheel, with the engine running. He waved at me jauntily as I approached, his mouth pursed under his elegant little moustache, his eyes naughty under his arched black eyebrows. He was nattily dressed for the wedding in an open-throated shirt, starchily white and obviously new.

Chuy watched from the door, gave me a nod, and then vanished inside. I knew, as she did, that there would be no Coras at this wedding.

There were already four pretty mestiza girls standing up in the back of the pickup, all in modish dresses from Tepic and all with soft blue makeup framing their bright, dark eyes.

I was surprised to see that Arcelia's Luz was not among them. If there was a chance to go somewhere, I thought, she would take it. She had ridden to El Cerro the other day and back again with José. Arcelia had railed at her.

"What do you mean, vagabonding around like that!" Arcelia had said. "Just like a man!"

Luz had looked sulky and had said nothing.

The girls who were there helped me climb up into the back of the pickup with them.

As we waited for Don Basilio and the bishop, there was a pitapat of tiny feet and a whisper, just a whisper. Passing by the atrium were three little burros, each with a feathery load of dried corn foliage on its back, fodder for mules in the corral half a kilometer up The Street in Front of the Church. As I watched them and listened to the rustle of the delicate dry leaves, I had a moment of compassion for my successors on Madison Avenue. They were probably at that moment straining at their desks for the bright new selling idea required every day.

Don Basilio and the bishop emerged from the burros' door into the atrium, Don Basilio carrying the suitcase that I knew contained the bishop's ecclesiastical requisites. Don Basilio slid the suitcase into the back of the pickup truck and climbed up himself, while the bishop scolded me for not sitting in the front seat. Don Basilio finally persuaded him to take his proper place beside José, and we rattled off toward the river.

We splashed and rocked across the ford to the other side, where two of Don Basilio's big sons were waiting with six big milk cans of water.

Downriver, the new bridge was near completion. The concrete foundation on the Jesús María side was built up some fifteen feet, with a superstructure of steel above it. It was apparently going to be a footbridge, a suspension bridge, to swing high above the river, hair-raising in an April wind.

The big sons loaded the cans into the back of the pickup and jumped in themselves, along with Don Basilio and the pretty girls. There was no room for me. I slid over the milk cans and into the seat between the bishop and José, and we labored up the switchback and took off for the wedding.

When, after the usual terrifying ride, we finally arrived at the rancho, it appeared that no preparations had been started at all. The ground in front of the cook house was littered with bottle caps and gum wrappers. Two men with their hats on were delicately slicing paper-thin strips of meat from a carcass hanging from the limb of a scraggly tree beside the sleeping house. Don Basilio had, indeed, killed a cow. Somebody had rigged up a line from the house to another tree, and the men were hanging up the meat to dry. The sow, turkey, and chickens were nowhere in sight.

Doña Dora greeted us, affable but cool. Her big sons wrestled the milk cans out of the back of the Datsun, Don Basilio slid out the suitcase, the pretty girls jumped down, and José spun the Datsun around in a whirl of dust and headed down the mountain to fetch more guests.

I followed along behind as Don Basilio deferentially escorted the bishop to a structure a little way down the road. It was a large, open-sided shelter with uprights made of tree trunks with forks at the top to hold long beams, also the trunks of trees. Over the beams was corrugated roofing, nicely laid on. Don Basilio had built the shelter for the wedding, I heard him tell the bishop. On one side, suspended from the roof and facing inside, was a large sign commemorating the completion of the road to Jesús María.

BY ORDER OF THE PRESIDENT OF THE REPUBLIC, it read, THE SECRETARIAT OF PUBLIC WORKS BUILT THIS ROAD WITH HAND LABOR TO THE COMMUNITY OF JESÚS MARÍA. LENGTH 6.45 KILOMETERS

This was where the wedding was to be consecrated, right in front of the sign.

Don Basilio had improvised an altar with wooden planks laid on two piles of Pepsi crates, nine crates to the pile. The bishop, still in his brown Franciscan habit, smoothed an embroidered altar cloth over the rough wooden boards as reverently as if he were in the most elegant cathedral in Mexico. He drew a tall white candle out of the suitcase, and a plastic drinking glass. Don Basilio came with a Fanta bottle, almost full, and his knife. The bishop screwed the candle into the bottle, sliced a little hole in the bottom of the plastic glass and slipped it over the tip of the candle to protect the small flame from the wind.

The wine was in a medicine bottle, but the bishop had brought his embossed gold chalice and a covered gold vessel for the Host. After he had placed his missal gently on the left side of the altar, he went outside and sat on a log, patient and majestic as always, contemplating the drying field beside the line of poinciana trees Don Basilio had planted beside the road.

Back at the rancho, I discovered that the men were still picking strips of beef off the now reduced carcass and hanging them on the line. I took pictures. There was activity around the cook house I hadn't seen before. Women inside it, women I recognized as being from two and three hours away, were chummily preparing food. One was grinding chile on a stone mortar. Another staggered in with an enormous cauldron of slivered beef, already cooked on a campfire alongside the kareton. Three women were behind the stove flipping tortillas. I took pictures.

More guests arrived, some on foot, some on mules that they tethered under the poinciana trees. José brought another truckload from Jesús María. Padre Domingo trotted in on his mule from doctoring a sick girl down on the far side of the mountain. I went out to meet him. He was scowling over the leisurely preparations.

"This people is always so late," he fussed in English, tying his ugly little mule to a fence post.

Then he grinned at me and trudged down the road to salute the bishop. Presently, in his own brown Franciscan habit, he was sitting beside the bishop on the log, contemplating the poincianas and tapping his foot.

I got tired of taking pictures and found a chair to sit in, in the shade. It was November. The fierceness of the sun had abated a little, but it was still hot at midday. The mountains were golding over. The wildflowers had burned up, and the grass around them was like straw, but the vermilion flycatcher was still darting out from his post and darting back again.

Preparations were beginning to accelerate a little. Two of the pretty girls from Jesús María had found brooms and were sweeping up the gum wrappers and bottle caps from in front of the cook house. Don Basilio and two of his sons fabricated a long table of rough planks on packing boxes as soon as the ground was swept clean. A couple of newly arrived women guests flicked tablecloths onto the table, tablecloths embroidered in colors, one with a border six inches wide.

In the windowless adobe storeroom attached to the kitchen, I caught a glimpse of the bride. Another of the girls from Jesús María had started the elaborate task of piling her hair into big hollow rolls on top of her head.

Doña Dora came out of the cook house to survey the table. "Your daughter is going to look lovely," I told her.

Doña Dora looked offended. "She is not my daughter," she said tartly. "The groom is my son."

The women in the cook house stirred rice and flipped more tortillas. Don Basilio's sons made benches along the sides of the table with planks laid on oil cans. I started taking pictures again.

The wedding had been scheduled for noon.

At two o'clock, Don Basilio brought Padre Domingo down from the log to the storeroom to hear the confessions of the wedding party. The bride, now in her wedding gown and with a fillet of blue plastic flowers supporting her elaborate coiffure, was the first to confess. Then she slipped out through the narrow door, and, one by one, the others slipped in.

To my surprise, the bride was not in white but in blue. Light, shiny blue. I had seen her before, in church, perhaps, or in Chela's store. She looked fatter than I remembered her, but the blue became her. How nice, I thought, that a Mexican girl could get married in a pretty color if she liked, instead of conventional white. And what a shame that her eyes were red. She had been crying. I wondered if Padre Domingo had been rough with her. She did not want me to photograph her.

At 2:30, two and a half hours after the scheduled time, the bride in blue, the groom in clean, dark trousers and a new white shirt, Don Basilio and Doña Dora, the pretty girls from Tepic, and we, the other guests, tramped down the dusty road to the shelter. The bishop was splendid in his silken vestments. Padre Domingo had put on a white surplice to serve as altar boy. Someone had laid a green blanket on the ground in front of the altar. The wedding party knelt on it. The men took off their hats. I put more film in my camera.

The young couple were kneeling in front of the altar when Padre Domingo stepped out from behind it and stood over the girl.

"I saw your father this morning," he said. "He sent his blessing in spite of the evil you did. You should go to your father and ask his blessing in person," he continued harshly. "And on your knees."

It appeared that I was the only person present to be horrified. Padre Domingo retreated, and the bishop, in his deep, kind voice, spoke the opening words of the wedding ceremony. Vows were exchanged, rings and money blessed, the rope of blossoms placed over the shoulders of the young couple, and the Mass celebrated.

The guests then embraced the bride and groom and filed back with them to the rancho.

Padre Domingo packed up the churchly treasures. The bishop, once more in his brown Franciscan habit, boarded the pickup truck and drove off with José, down, down the mountainside. Padre Domingo mounted his mule again and took off to marry another couple an hour and a half away. I stayed for the fiesta.

As the only gringa present and the official photographer, I ate at the first table with the wedding party. We worked our way quickly through the broth and rice and slivered beef cooked with chile, then toasted the bride with anise in plastic cups. The men all ate with their hats on—big, and white, and becoming.

As soon as we had finished, we rose to make room for the next shift while the women washed our dishes in the cook house. The second table included the musicians. There were five of them: two violins, one guitar, a mandolin, and a bass. After they had eaten, they began to make music.

One of the violinists, in a melancholy tenor, sang the endless verses of Mexican country songs, the other musicians accompanying him and punctuating the end of each verse with an instrumental furbelow.

It was late afternoon when the last guest was fed and the benches carried out to a patch of well-watered ground. Don Basilio had sprinkled it from a pail of water while the guests were eating. The girls seated themselves in a row on one of the benches. The musicians switched to dance music, and the bride and groom took a stately turn around the earthen dance floor before sitting down, side by side, in the only two chairs in the rancho.

It was night when I started down the mountain in the cab of the Datsun beside the smiling José. There was no moon. The lights of the truck seemed dim. José drove fast, skidding around the turns. I knew he was going to go straight back up the mountain. The dancing would go on all night, he told me, and José was a very good dancer.

He let me out at the foot of the hill that led up to Jesús María and to my little house. By the feeble light of a flashlight he loaned me, I threaded my way up the again dry brush to Jesús María and my little house, thinking about the wedding. I was perplexed.

The next morning, I sought out Chela.

"The wedding wasn't at the bride's house," I said. "It was at the groom's."

"Of course," Chela said, as if she were not at all interested.

"But with us it's always the father of the bride who gives the wedding," I persisted. "Sometimes he even pays for the dresses of the bridesmaids."

"It's different here," Chela said, examining the gizzard of a chicken she was cutting up.

"But, Chela," I said, "the bride's parents didn't even come to the wedding."

"So?" Chela said. She wasn't helping me at all.

"The bride wore blue," I said, trying to distract her.

"Of course," Chela said. "She had to."

"She had to! What do you mean, Chela? Why?"

"The bride was not a señorita," Chela said primly.

It took me a minute to understand what Chela, in such a genteel manner, was telling me. I guessed that she had not said "virgin" because of its religious connotations. I recalled that the bride, in her blue wedding dress, did look fatter than I remembered.

"She ran away from home to live with Don Basilio's son," Chela said.

So that was why Arcelia's Luz had not been allowed to go to the wedding, I thought to myself. Out loud I said, "So that's why she wasn't married in her father's house."

"No," said Chela patiently. "The wedding is always the affair of the groom. He buys the wedding dress, and his parents give the fiesta after the ceremony."

"With us," I said, "it's always the bride's parents who give the wedding." It seemed important to make her understand.

"Not with us," said Chela.

"Not even when the wedding is here, in the church?" I persisted.

"No. The father and mother go to the church with sour faces. After the wedding, they don't go to the fiesta. They go home to sulk."

"Why?"

"Because they are losing a daughter. She goes to live with the groom's family."

"But the bride's parents didn't even go to the wedding." I couldn't get over it.

"The two families are not friends."

"But who are the bride's parents?" I asked. "Who is the bride's father?"

Chela told me the bride's father's name. I knew him. He was a charming man, but young girls had to keep out of his way.

As soon as I caught up with Padre Domingo, I tackled him.

"Why were you so rough with that poor girl?" I asked him.

"She ran away from home," he said. "She ran away to live with that boy."

"But to tell her that she should go on her knees to her father!" I protested. "Her father is a scamp. He's charming, but a scamp, a real scamp."

"Of course, he's a scamp," Padre Domingo said. "Everybody knows that. But he's her father. And someday, Catareen, you will learn," he said severely, "that this is Mexico."

10

Candles Light the First Posada

Christmas came, as it always does, before I was ready for it. My monthly week in Guadalajara had stretched out into two, what with frantically sealing Christmas cards and wrapping trifles to mail to my children and grandchildren in the States.

It was the middle of December before I finally landed in El Cerro and clattered down to Jesús María in the Datsun.

After storing my belongings in my little house, I went into the store to share a rib-cracking hug with Chela and to marvel at her new Christmas merchandise and to exclaim over the decorations in her *sala*, her living room, now festooned with tinsel and hung with every tawdry Christmas bell, and to the curato to pay my respects to the bishop and to find out what ugly job Padre Domingo had for me this time.

The bishop had mounted his big, heavyweight mule and had plodded off on a pre-Christmas visit to some of the smaller settlements in the mountains roundabout. Padre Domingo was sitting on the ground, out behind the kitchen, chipping the bottoms off liter-size glass jars. Another robust young man was with him, also chipping. Padre Domingo introduced him. He was the new friar, Fray Nicolas, almost nattily dressed in a clean white shirt and clean khaki pants. Padre Domingo, as usual, was in a disreputable brown shirt hanging out over smudged white Cora pants. They were both surrounded by jars and broken glass.

"What on earth?" I asked them.

"The *posada*," the padre said, giving me his three-cornered grin.

"The posada?"

The year before, in Guadalajara, I had attended a posada, the annual ceremony commemorating the biblical search for an inn. That posada was in the patio of a big, pretentious house. The cold had been paralyzing. We had all worn heavy coats over our evening clothes. The decorations had been elaborate, the outdoor buffet lavish, and the few guests from the States had shivered through four or five Christmas carols. Then we had all hurried home to go to bed and get warm.

At that posada, I hadn't seen a single glass jar, mutilated or otherwise.

"The posada?" I was quite understandably bewildered.

"You'll see," the padre said and grinned again.

I did see, just a few days later, the first posada of the nine posadas that would lead up to Christmas.

It started in the late afternoon, after the end of the Rosary. The children filed out of the church singing. First came the acolytes, all who ever served at the altar. They were in mufti now: clean shirts, new trousers, worn huaraches. Each carried what appeared to be a hurricane lamp, lighted.

Next straggled out the youngest children, herded along by a couple of cheerful nuns who were visiting the curato.

Then came Mary and Joseph, tiny figurines on a rough wooden litter with carrying shafts before and behind.

Carrying in front was Macario, a little cross-eyed mestizo. Carrying in back was Anastasia, a pretty little Cora all covered up in a fancy black lace mantilla. Her small, tidy feet were bare.

Padre Domingo and the new friar followed Mary and Joseph out of the church.

Then came the women, head and shoulders swathed in their speckled black rebozos, I in my woolen shawl.

Last of all came the few old men who regularly turned out for the Rosary.

The little procession sang its way over the sandy atrium, out through the open gate and onto the rocky road. It turned to the right and strung out along The Street in Front of the Church, between the rows of little mestizo houses, singing all the way.

It was still light when we left the church, but evening comes fast in the mountains. The hills darkened, brown into purple, sand into blue. The sky lightened over the penciled brows of the mountaintops. By the side of the road, the trunk of a palo verde glowed acid green in the fading light. Hens floundered up to roost in its branches. Suddenly the sky darkened, and it was night.

Two guitarists joined the procession, Don David and Don Ricardo, the same Don Ricardo who had helped me across the river on the bridge of boulders. They softly picked out the plaintive melody, so much gentler then the songs we sang in church.

On goes Joseph. On goes Mary.
On to Bethlehem, walking night and day.

I suddenly realized what the altar boys were carrying. They were not hurricane lamps. They were the glass jars from which Padre Domingo and Fray Nicolas had been hacking off the bottoms. The metal tops of the jars had been nailed to wooden paddles. The upended jars had then been screwed into the tops, which served as bases for the candles. The bottomless jars now made chimneys that let air in to the brightly burning candles. The candlelight illuminated the murderously jagged edges of the jars.

On sang the procession, from time to time augmented as one or another black-shrouded woman and white-hatted man drifted out from nowhere to stumble along in the darkness. Chela and Don Paco were not among them. Business was brisk back in the store with the Coras in from their ranchos.

At last one of the nuns and three young girls slipped into a house. Macario and Anastasia, with Mary and Joseph, stopped in front of the door. The procession came to an untidy halt, and the singing outside changed.

We come from a long hard journey.
We implore a refuge where we can rest.

The nun and the girls sang from inside the window, the only window in the house.

Who imprudently comes in the night
To our very door thus to molest us?

Their voices floated out, sounding young and innocent for the rude words they were singing.

The crowd outside commiserated.

> Poor, poor pilgrims
> Who on alien soil
> Go disconsolate
> Looking for a shelter.

The faces of the little acolytes gleamed in the light of the candles. The procession moved on, and the song continued.

> On goes Joseph with his beloved wife
> Sad and afflicted, from here to another inn.

It had turned cold—not nearly as cold as that night of the posada in Guadalajara, but cold. The women wrapped themselves tighter in their black rebozos, I in my shawl.

The stars came out, millions of them, stabbing through the darkness of the sky. Don Ricardo picked out the sad little melody, Don David embroidered it with a delicate obbligato.

The song seemed endless, but the faithful knew all the words. For Mary and Joseph they twice more pleaded asylum and twice more were rebuffed. Then, finally, at the very end of The Street in Front of the Church, Mary and Joseph were at last invited in. The gate swung open on its hand-hewn wooden hinge, and we all surged into the yard of Don Felicitas and Doña Alicia, still singing.

The altar boys marched into the house with their lighted candles. Padre Domingo shepherded the little children out of the way to let Macario and Anastasia follow with Mary and Joseph. The song went on and on.

The house was one of the finest in Jesús María, for Don Felicitas was rich. He had cattle and mules, goats, sheep, and even a horse or two. The house was of adobe with a tiled roof and a brick floor, with a front porch that served as a sitting room, and a separate little adobe house for cooking. Flowering laurels and bougainvilleas were planted haphazardly between the house and the low stone wall. Even in the dark, the place was inviting.

The room with the door onto the porch had been readied for the holy guests. It was empty, except for a table covered with an elaborately embroidered tablecloth. Stretched on the wall behind the table was another cloth to which Doña Alicia had pinned a dozen Christmas cards, all with religious pictures, many obviously saved from Christmases long past.

Macario and Anastasia carefully mounted the steps and edged their way through the door. They slid the litter onto the table, blessed themselves, drew a breath of relief, and made a dive for the door. The altar boys put their candles on the floor in front of the table and slipped out of the room.

The rest of us filed into the room and out again. The singing went on, then prayers led by Fray Nicolas, then more singing. At last the devotions came to an end, and it was time for the fun to start.

Don Felicitas herded all the children out the gate. He had already strung up a rope between two trees in the yard, a rope well over his head. Fray Nicolas tied a lighter rope around the neck of the first piñata. It was a small piñata, just a little clay pot with paper flowers on top. Doña Elena had brought it to the posada apologetically. She was a small, gentle woman. Chela told me that she had only six hens and that they didn't lay much. It was obvious that her small piñata couldn't hold many peanuts or much hard candy.

Fray Nicolas handled it with great respect, however, hunkering down to tie the thin, strong line tightly around the neck of the pot. Then he stood up and threw the loose end of the line up over the rope, and Don Felicitas opened the gate to let the children come in. While Padre Domingo was blindfolding a little four–year–old boy named Cirilo, the friar was testing the line, pulling on it and letting it go slack to raise and lower the piñata. The children thronged around in a big circle, squealing.

They kept on squealing while Cirilo tried to smash the piñata. Padre Domingo had given him a baseball bat, turned him completely around, faced him toward the piñata, and then abandoned him. While Fray Nicolas played the piñata up and down and Cirilo swung harmlessly, the spectators screamed advice. "Higher! Lower! More to the left!"

At last, Cirilo's turn was up. Padre Domingo took off his blindfold and hugged him, and then tied the handkerchief around the eyes of Anastasia, the little Cora girl who had carried one end of the litter. She threw her mananita to one of the laughing nuns and began swinging the bat wildly as soon as Padre Domingo had her in place.

I realized with a shock that she was the only Cora at the posada. The rest were all mestizos.

Anastasia struck out, as Cirilo had done, and three more children batted away at the elusive little piñata until, finally, one hit home and the peanuts and candies showered down on the ground. There were not a great many, but all the children scrambled for them by the light of Doña Alicia's flashlight.

The second piñata was big, at least two feet high. I wondered at the stamina of whoever had brought the big clay jar from Tepic. It was heavy, and the shops that carried bowls and jugs of clay were on the far side of town from the airport. Air freight would have cost something, too, and it must have taken hours to decorate it here in Jesús María.

This second piñata was a duck, each tissue-paper feather glued on separately. Its head was made from a carton pasted over with colored paper, its beak apparently cut from a fruit-juice can. The third was a clown. Both were so big they held a whole handful of goodies for every shrieking child.

After all the piñatas had been broken and the children had quieted down, Doña Alicia distributed goodies to all of us out of a big pink plastic washtub: peanuts and animal crackers in little brown paper bags. Then we all said our good-nights and picked our way out to the cobbled road.

The singing started up again, but now it was a merry song: "*Navidad, Navidad*," "Christmas, Christmas," sung to the tune of "Jingle Bells." The guitarists were strumming and thumping now, and a few of the children were clapping out the rhythm. I saw that Fray Nicolas was shepherding little Anastasia to get her back safely to her Cora family.

The moon came up to light our way home.

Back in the room with the Christmas cards and the candles, Don Felicitas and Doña Alicia were keeping an all-night vigil. They had given Mary and Joseph the place where, on ordinary nights, they had their own bed. On this night of their posada, there was no room for them to sleep.

11

It's Safer on the Roof

The posada had been attended almost exclusively by mestizos. Then came Christmas, and both Coras and mestizos kissed the statue of the baby Jesus. The next big event was a Cora fiesta. It was memorable for me because it was the first full-dress fiesta I had ever seen and because at the end of it, on New Year's Day, an Indian knocked me down.

It was my own fault that I got knocked down. Chela had urged me to watch with her and Paco from the roof of Mario's store.

"This affair gets rough toward the end," she told me.

But there I was, right on the edge of the action, taking pictures, pictures, pictures. I didn't even see what hit me, or who.

It was the annual fiesta celebrating the changeover of the tribal government. The Coras were bowing out the old Authorities and welcoming in the new. They had selected a new governor, a new vice governor, a new judge, new surrogates for the outlying settlements, new native police. The fiesta, Chela assured me, would be spectacular.

The town filled up with Coras from everywhere, more Coras than I had ever seen before. They trickled down the switchback on the hill that loomed up behind Chela's compound, whole families of them, some on foot, some on muleback. They waded across the river where it curved around the Cora houses down at the bottom end of town. They filtered down out of the mountains to the north, passing a little scornfully through the rows of mestizo houses upriver, on their way to leave their offerings in the church and then to go on to meet their friends down in the Cora part of town.

They came from all over the mountains on the other side of the river, too, crossing on the new suspension footbridge, leaving their mules behind.

The bridge was a frail, spidery span of metal frame and wooden flooring, flung high above the water from one side of the river to the other. Government engineers had appeared from nowhere when the pick–and–shovel work was done. The bridge was not strong enough to support a burro or quite wide enough for two people to walk abreast. The Coras, in single file, padded across it warily, for it rocked with every footstep and swung with the slightest breeze.

There was not a Cora house in Jesús María without its nightly complement of blanketed bodies asleep on the floor. It was easy to understand why: not only was this an important event in the life of the tribe and a splendid chance to make one's peace with the santitos in the church, it was, as Chela had said, a marvelous show.

It started with the Moors.

One night there came floating down from the mesa of San Miguel a faint, insistent drumming and, with it, a soft, silvery piped melody, repeated over and over. The next morning, over the brow of the mesa, appeared the musicians. There were three drummers and one piper with his slender, handmade flute. Drumming and piping, they marched sturdily down the lava flow.

Right behind them came the Moors on their ponies, eight slim young men in white muslin trousers and wildly colored shirts. They sat erect in their saddles, their big hats shadowing their faces, their reins held high. The ponies picked their way carefully down the treacherous descent.

In single file they took a turn around the town, fetching up at last in the big sandy square Chela told me was their own parade ground. There the drummers and the piper, still drumming and piping, took shelter from the tropical sun under the overhanging roof of one of the little houses flanking the field. The ponies, at a sedate hand canter, began what turned out to be an almost interminable horse quadrille.

They formed a circle, turned and cantered to the center, fanned out to the sides, formed a square and crossed corner to corner, one horse circling another before cantering back. The riders sat quietly, their faces expressionless, their eyes straight ahead.

From then on, the equestrian square dance almost never stopped, except for brief respites when the riders filed back up to eat or when, at night, the field was at last a big, dark smudge under a skyful of stars.

The Moors had been cantering for several days before the dancers came down from the mesa. They came at midnight, a moonless midnight. The biggest church bell started booming. Rockets began to hiss in the atrium and thunder in the sky. Over the brow of the mesa and down the lava flow, I could see the flickering light of torches. The "Urracas," the magpie jays, were coming, the aristocrats of Indian dancers.

I was waiting for them in the atrium. Chela had told me when they would come. I slipped inside the church, slid into a pew, and hunched down to keep warm. Scorching as the sun could be in the daytime, the night was cold as only tropical nights can be.

The church smelled of incense. The Coras had draped swaths of wide, white lace from the skylights in the high, vaulted ceiling to spikes in the walls. There were fresh roses in fruit–juice cans on the old altar. Slender tapers in the high brass chandelier gave a wavering light.

Another fiesta was coming on the heels of this one, the fiesta of the Three Wise Men. Two of them, Balthasar and Gaspar, exquisite little porcelain figures, were already on a low table in front of the new altar. Melchior, the third Wise Man, was unaccountably missing–lost or stolen, Chela didn't know which.

Two Cora women, their skirts spread out around them, were sitting on the floor on either side of the table to keep the incense burning in the crude clay bowls.

Don Nazario, his fine, chiseled old face absolutely expressionless, his arms, as usual, folded on his chest, stood erect and motionless in the far corner of the church.

Fray Nicolas had pushed the benches back against the side walls to make room for the dancers, all the way from the big open doors to the small low table in front of the altar. They came into church dancing, a delicate, precise, courtly dance, with sandaled feet slapping, patting, caressing the floor. They were accompanied by a single violinist making a rhythmic pattern for the dance with dissonant chords and slippery glissandos.

The lateness of the hour, the dimness of the light, the smoke of the incense, and the strangeness of the music all combined to lend an unearthly quality to the dance and the dancers. I watched them fascinated.

I had read how, in other places in the west of Mexico, the Jesuit missionaries had found the Indians dancing where once they had had their idols. Do come into the church, the Jesuits had invited them, and dance there for the Virgin.

The Coras now were dancing in the church, dancing with rapt faces, dancing their religion. But what religion was it, really? The religion the Jesuits had taught them centuries ago and that the Franciscans were selflessly practicing now? The cynical anthropologists said no. How was I to know?

And how was anyone to know from where came the inspiration for their costumes? Over bright, printed kerchiefs that covered their heads and shoulders, they wore crowns, globes covered with paper carnations in pink, and red, and blue, and white. Insets of tiny mirrors glinted in the candlelight. Slender, deep-blue feathers, tipped with white down, thrust straight up from the flowery crowns, tail feathers of the *urraca*, the magpie jay whose name the dancers bore. Multicolored fishnet dripped over their faces. Satin ribbons in yellow, red, blue, and purple dripped down their backs.

Each, in his right hand, carried a rattle made from a small gourd from the calabash tree. In his left hand, he held a three-pronged scepter, which he slowly waved back and forth as he danced.

With the dancers came a mascot and a buffoon.

The mascot was a little girl, not more than five years old. She, too, wore a flower crown and carried a rattle and a scepter. She stood in the midst of the dancers, who gently pushed her from one place to another, where she docilely stood waiting to be pushed again.

The buffoon appeared actually to be the ringmaster. He wore a mask with a long gringo nose and a long mane of blonde horsehair, and he carried a bullwhip, which he cracked from time to time.

He cracked it gently when it was time for the dancers to leave the church. Patting, slapping, caressing the floor with their sandaled feet, they danced out of the door, turning again and again to bow deeply over a bent leg. The little girl trudged obediently after them.

There were two more groups of dancers: one group of young men, tough, exuberant, and showy; the other group of older men, awkward and sad. Finally, the last of the dancers disappeared out of the door.

The church was empty now except for the two women tending the incense (replacements had come in during the dancing), six Coras who were asleep in the pews, and Don Nazario, still standing erect in the dark corner of the church. He moved out deliberately, took from the wall a long slender pole tipped with a nosegay of fresh flowers, dipped them in the bowl of water in front of the Wise Men, and then raised them to extinguish the candles in the chandelier. I followed him out of the church.

The Urracas came down from the mesa of San Miguel the next morning. I was eating breakfast with Don Paco.

"What wonderful photographs those dancers will make," I said, as their escort of pipe and drummers passed the house.

"Photographs?" Chela, flipping tortillas, sounded doubtful.

"But the Coras like me to photograph them," I said complacently. "You know how they're always asking me to."

So I slung my camera strap over my shoulder and loped off to work in Padre Domingo's clinic. The padre was away, and it seemed as if all of the tribe were in town and they all had cut feet, or bad colds, or diarrhea. There was plenty to do.

I managed to step outside in the middle of the morning. The Urracas were patting and slapping their way to the ramada in front of the Health Center, the big, square shelter with its permanent frame of pine trunks and its temporary roof of fresh oak branches. The light was perfect. I dropped to one knee and started to focus my camera. The buffoon saw me. With his blonde horsehair streaming out behind his long-nosed mask, he ran toward me, snapping his bullwhip at me. I made a clumsy but hasty retreat.

"Possibly, if you ask permission . . . ," Chela tentatively suggested at dinnertime.

I stole a few minutes off the next morning and braved Don Arnulfo in the Presidencia. He was at his desk again in the huge, gloomy room, looking as square and solid as ever.

"I can't give you permission," he said cheerfully. "You will have to ask the governor, Don Teodulo."

"Not Don Teodulo." I quailed a little. "Is he the governor?"

"Yes," said Don Arnulfo. "He is the governor, and this is a tribal affair."

I went looking for Don Teodulo that afternoon. I remembered his dark, brooding face as he had sung through the night in a "soul-calling" ritual, calling back the soul of a man who had died so his family and friends could bid him good-bye. As I scrambled up the lava flow to the mesa of San Miguel, I kept enjoining myself to be brave and resourceful.

Six or seven Coras were standing around in front of one of the small, brown, stone houses. I asked for Don Teodulo. Everybody laughed, and one of the women pointed to a man with a lined, clever face, who was throwing a ball in the air and catching it, pretending I wasn't there. He looked quite different from the sinister Cora I remembered.

I made my plea. Don Teodulo refused me. The others kept on laughing. Don Teodulo sobered.

"Nobody takes pictures of the dancers," he said, dropping the ball into his woven bag. "Nobody."

"It would be best if you put your camera away," Chuy said when I told her.

I still watched the dancers whenever I could. If I had a few free minutes, I would slip into the church. There were often a few Coras asleep in the pews. The dancers were getting tired. The women tending the incense left the church wearily when a new pair came to relieve them. From time to time, when there were no dancers, a Cora would pad down to the Wise Men to kneel and leave his offerings. Often he would have his wife with him and a child or two. There was a bowl of water on the table with white flowers in it. The man would sprinkle the heads of his wife and children and then his own head. After a little while, they would all rise and file out of the church.

The spicy, sweet perfume of the incense always filled the church.

Other things kept happening. There were feasts in the ramada two days in a row. Coras brought benches, goodness knows from where. They brought planks and sawhorses to make tables. Big clay pots materialized on the ground beside the ramada, and Cora women sat down beside them, their full flowered skirts spread out around them, their tight basque waists white for the fiesta. The pots held chunks of beef in its own brown broth, rice, beans, and *atole,* a drink rather like a liquid cornstarch pudding. There were huge baskets of charcoal–gray tortillas made from blue Indian corn. It all smelled delicious.

The Cora Authorities sat down at the tables in the ramada. So did the dancers, after carefully hanging their crowns on pegs in the pine uprights. Women served the food in plastic bowls, and a group of men who were apparently designated to serve literally ran from the pots to the tables.

There was a special Mass, too, which almost all of the Coras, surprisingly, attended. The bishop celebrated it with fatherly affection. With his kind, deep voice rolling out over the bare heads of the men and the speckled rebozos of the women, he enunciated each word so clearly that all the Coras, and even I, could understand.

The Cora orchestra played Cora music in the choir loft. It was fascinating music, gloriously discordant, with several violins and a big bass drum.

Early one morning, five Cora men and two boys appeared on the switchback behind my house with several well–loaded burros tiptoeing down the trail.

"Bananas for the fiesta," Chela told me.

The little caravan swerved off the switchback onto the short trail that led directly to San Miguel and disappeared behind the thorn trees.

The Moors kept on cantering in their parade ground, the slim young men sitting straight and collected in their saddles. Four of them, a couple of days before the change of government, appeared on the field with tall turbans of paper flowers and with kerchiefs drawn over their mouths and noses like visors. They carried white banners dotted with pink pompoms and took the lead in all the intricate figures of the continuing horse quadrille.

I loved to watch the Moors and longed to photograph them. No–

body told me I couldn't, so I finally slung my idle camera around my neck and marched to the parade ground.

A small spotted pig accompanied me.

I found a splendid place to photograph and had the flower turbans in focus when a couple of young Coras swayed up, each with a bottle.

As Don Arnulfo had observed, Prohibition did not apply to fiestas.

"Have a drink," one said, holding out his bottle unsteadily.

They were very drunk, so I let my camera dangle and took a token swig, not wishing to offend them.

"I'd like to photograph the Moors," I confessed, as I wiped the mouth of the bottle with my sleeve, the way I had seen them do in western movies.

"Have a drink," the other young man said, as he hospitably pressed his bottle into my hand. I took another sip and wiped the bottle.

"I'd like to photograph the Moors," I said again.

"Oh, no," the first young man said, wagging his head.

"Nobody photographs the Moors," the second young man said owlishly. "Nobody."

I was about to give up when I saw Don Nicomedes advancing toward me along the edge of the field. I knew Don Nicomedes well. I had taken care of his wife, who suffered a lot from rheumatism. I appealed to him.

"These young men say I can't photograph the Moors," I told him.

"Come along, Doña Cata. Let's go up to your house," Don Nicomedes said. "You don't want anything to do with these boys. They're drunk." Then, steering me gracefully up the hill, he said: "I don't see very well. I need glasses. Is it true that you have glasses?"

As I tried one pair of glasses after another on Don Nicomedes, I told him how I had been thwarted.

"You don't want to take pictures of the dancers or the Moors now," Don Nicomedes said soothingly. "Better to take pictures when the old government goes out and the new government comes in. That's more interesting, and I can give you permission for that. I will

become governor myself then," he said. "Perhaps you would care to
cooperate?"

By some miracle, I realized that this meant money.

"How much?" I asked.

He named a sum that was just a little more than the plane fare
from Guadalajara to Puerto Vallarta. How lucky could I be, I thought,
to know the new governor, and he so obliging.

I cooperated.

New Year's Day finally arrived. The actual change of government
was going to take place in the afternoon, in the big, bare space in
front of the ramada. I was there with my camera, legal at last.

First came the bearers bringing chairs, native ones made of palm
and otate, the Mexican bamboo. On the backs of the chairs were
somewhat scandalous little figurines made of tortilla dough. On each
seat was a crown made of the bananas I had seen the Coras bring in
on the burros. I took pictures.

Suddenly, from behind the ramada, there came running a group
of youths with reed "bulls" over their heads and backs, bulls complete with horns. More youths appeared, these on ponies galloping,
chasing the bulls. The people flanking the field ran screaming for
cover.

I took my place in front of a low stone wall and kept on shooting
pictures. Suddenly, something struck me on the chest, and I went
backward onto the rocks on the far side of the wall. A bull in a chile-
colored shirt had charged me, they told me later.

He didn't know I had cooperated.

I didn't see the actual change of government that first year. I was
in bed at the time, with Chela scolding me.

"This town is full of young Coras from all over the mountains,"
she said. "Coras who don't know you."

But she did tell me what I would have seen had I been there to
see it: how the bulls and the ponies would have run off the field with
the Moors decorously pattering behind and the dancers following;
how the men of the new government would then have filed on and
halted in midfield, while the Urracas danced and bowed before them;
how the bearers of the chairs would have crowned the new incum-
bents with the banana crowns; how, after a little ceremony, the bulls

would have reappeared with the horsemen chasing them; and how, finally, the Moors and the new Authorities would have formed a procession and filed off the field in the direction of the mesa of San Miguel.

I have absolutely no pictures of the change of government. I saved my camera when the Cora knocked me down, but all the pictures I had taken that afternoon were on one frame. My camera had jammed.

As soon as I was limber enough to scale a ladder, I climbed up to see whether or not I might be able to get pictures of the fiesta the following year. I sadly decided that I couldn't. There wasn't a single decent camera angle from the roof of Mario's store.

12

When the River Rises

We had already had our annual unexpected winter rain in January, when we were supposed to have it. The flood came in February.

The rain came without warning. One day the sky was hot and blue. The next day it was silver and the rain was falling.

It was a soft rain, a gentle rain, a rain that scarcely made a whisper on my red tile roof. It drifted down softly, gently, all day and all night, all the next day and all the next night, and so on, day after day and night after night. It rained without stopping. It rained as if it would never stop. It rained for six days, and then my roof fell in.

Chela cried. She loved the little house. She had built it for a nephew who had since deserted the Sierra for Colorado and an American bride.

"It's almost new," she said, crying. "It's only six years old. It shouldn't fall down, not yet."

Adobe houses do fall down sometimes, in the rain. Arcelia's house on the hill above us had fallen down when a stream of water suddenly swept down the hill. The adobes had melted. The ridgepole had slid down. The ribs and reeds and tiles of the roof had settled over the muddy rubble into a dismal pile. Only the door frame stood staunch and solid through the deluge and after.

That had happened in the wet season, though, last summer. Here we were in the middle of winter, in "the dries."

Little by little, the river began to rise.

Every day it spread out a little more. On the third day, it was still within the banks it reached in the summertime, but it was surging along, swollen, ugly, brown, and terribly fast.

On the fourth day, it swamped the water holes.

Juana came with the two empty buckets Filemon had picked up earlier. "Why didn't Filemon bring me my water?" I asked her after the customary embraces. He always brought it every morning, the two buckets slopping over a little as they swung from his shoulder yoke.

"Filemon is at home." Juana said. She was Chela's next-older sister, the one married to Don Gustavo, my guide on the mule trips to El Cerro and my caretaker at large. Her sweet, patient face was pale this morning, and her hair, usually so tidily twisted into a bun, was wet and wisping a little.

"Filemon dug three water holes, and the river rose and filled up all of them," she said. "Filemon is at home crying."

After embracing Juana again, I put the two buckets under a drip from the roof.

The mestizo houses on the ledge upriver were all above the water. So was the church. Down on the flats below the church, Don Dionisio grew his peanuts. Don Pedro had a circular stone wall for containing the few steers he brought down from the rancho. From behind the church, on the lip of the ledge, one could see down to the flats and over the river to the steep hills on the other side with their scattering of huts shaggily thatched with grass. Starting on the fourth day, one man, two men, three men in their big white hats stood motionless and silent on the edge of the ledge behind the church, watching the flats and the river.

All the world was wet. The earth was mud, adobe mud that sucked at our shoes and clung to their soles when we tried to scrape it off. The packed earth of Chela's patio turned into a shallow pond. The atrium of the church turned into a muddy lake. Little rivulets of water cut into the clay of the pathways. Our feet were always wet.

I wore a raincoat and carried an umbrella. My younger son, Mike, was visiting me. He wore a hooded waterproof nylon jacket, bright red. The other inhabitants of Jesús María, hardier than we, walked through the rain unprotected. The women covered their heads and shoulders with their speckled black rebozos. Three of the men had plastic covers for their hats. Nobody but us had a raincoat or an umbrella.

Every roof in town was leaking, including mine. On the fourth night, both Mike and I woke up with big drops of water falling on our faces. Our beds got wet. Our clothes got wet. Our towels got wet. Our firewood got wet, and there was no way to dry out anything.

Chela came staggering into the house with big plastic sheets to make a waterproof ceiling under the cheesecloth ceiling that kept the scorpions from falling on us. We stretched out the plastic, tied it to the ribs of the roof, and put buckets under the corners where the water would run off the plastic and onto the floor.

Before the sky had clouded over, a couple of innocents had limped into town: a longhaired boy from the States and a Mexican girl in a sari. They had wandered into our part of the Sierra by mistake. Somebody had told them about a fiesta in the Huichol zone. They had trustingly bought tickets to Santa Teresa, expecting to find Huichols there, but Santa Teresa is deep inside the Cora country. They were still trying to get to the Huichols. They were both barefoot, and their feet were sore. They had walked seven hours before they reached Jesús María.

Chela rented them a room, like all her rooms windowless and with a small door onto the patio. It started to rain the day after they arrived.

They were vegetarians, and there were no vegetables in Jesús María. I reluctantly produced hot chocolate, store cookies, peanut butter, and orange marmalade. The male innocent smiled beatifically and murmured, "Beautiful. Beautiful."

Our sterling young doctor in the Health Center had ordered Don Nicomedes to bring two of his grandchildren in for daily shots of antibiotics. The children were both dangerously sick with pneumonia.

As the governor of the tribe, Don Nicomedes was supposed to stay in Jesús María all of the time, but he complied with the doctor's command and then removed his family, grandchildren and all, to his house on top of one of the hills on the far side of the river. With the rain raining down and the trails running rivers, there was no hope of his bringing the children down to Jesús María again. Somebody had to cross the river, climb the hill, and give the shots to the children.

The doctor volunteered me.

My raincoat had gone spongy with the wet. My son Mike loaned me his red jacket. I was grateful that it had a hood. Also, the color was so bright that it would be easy to find me if I slipped off the trail.

Actually, it was fairly simple sliding down the path from the ledge, crossing the flats, and lurching across the river on the swaying new footbridge. The trail up to Don Nicomedes's house, however, was worse than the Coras who directed me had warned me. It was a long trail, too vertical for my taste, and obviously rough in the best weather. With the water cascading down it, the clay had turned to lard in some places and in some places to glue. It pulled off one of my shoes three times. By the time I finally reached the house, I was wet and exhausted and had mud in my shoes.

Don Nicomedes's house was built of rocks the old Indian way, with pebble fill and thatch of grass. It was a tiny house but solid.

Its one small room was full when I ducked in through the low, narrow door. In the darkness, I could see Don Nicomedes and his wife on the floor at the far end of the room. They were shelling corn. On a stool next to the door, one of their big sons was spinning wool. On the native bed, there were seven people: one grown man holding a baby, two daughters-in-law with small children in their laps, and a child of five lying down. A third son was sitting on a stool, playing plaintive Cora music on a violin. Into the reeds overhead were stuck the feathered arrows that protected the family from harm. The roof, I observed, was not leaking.

The son with the wool put his spindle on the dirt floor to get out the children's medicine. It was in a woven Cora bag hanging from a spike thrust between the stones of the wall. The family watched me impassively as I prepared the syringes. The bottoms of the baby and the child lying down were obligingly presented to me. The son with the violin, always watching me, played on.

It was warm and dry in the house, and I was wet and cold. I would have liked to stay a little longer, but there was no place to sit down.

I sloshed out through the yard and started to slide down the hill. Buds were showing on the bare branches of the thorn trees. On either side of the path, tiny plants were starting up, two little green leaves to each plant, the plants I had seen after the first rains in June. Only lacking were the tiny red velvet bugs that then had hustled over the wet ground between the newborn peanuts to proclaim that summer had come.

It was almost dark when I made it down to the footbridge. The river was snarling over the rocks. Swallows were flying low over the water.

On the fifth day, I wetly struggled up to Don Nicomedes's house again, but that was the last day I could give the shots. On the sixth day, the river burst its banks.

A number of us were watching on the lip of the ledge behind the church when it happened. Water began to seep onto the flats upriver. It pushed itself down surprisingly fast, smooth and brown. It deepened and pushed on, faster. It submerged Don Pedro's corral. Boulder by boulder, the wall tumbled, thundering as the water surged on.

"It's washing away the sand where I plant my peanuts," Don Dionisio observed mournfully.

Suddenly, on the far side of the river, seven Coras streaked into view, one behind the other, running down the trail. They were racing the river. They ran jolting across the footbridge and headed downriver to where the flats were still dry. The water reached there before they did, but they waded across it with the water swirling around their knees. We cheered when they reached dry land.

They were the last to cross the river. We were marooned.

The innocents stayed in their room, sitting on the wood-framed rawhide bed with their feet stretched out and their backs against the wall. Sometimes the boy played melancholy little tunes on his harmonica. Sometimes the girl sang sad little songs in what she said was Sanskrit. From time to time, I cooked oatmeal and ungraciously offered it to them. From time to time, they asked when the rain would stop.

The river kept rising, the rain kept raining, and on the seventh day my roof fell in.

I was filing my nails when it happened. For a couple of days, pieces of plaster had been falling off the wall from up near the roof in the other of my two rooms. Don Paco said not to worry.

"Plaster is falling off all over town," he said. "It's nothing to worry about."

All the same, as I sat there with my emery board, I began to worry a little. More and more plaster was falling, and oftener. I went to the door and called to Chela. She came out into the patio, took one look at my house, and began to scream. I went outside. The roof over the room with the falling plaster was sagging like the spine of a sway backed horse.

Don Paco strode out into the patio when he heard Chela scream. She pointed at the roof. He looked, looked again, and then crashed into my house. He yanked down the plastic sheets and the cheese-cloth ceiling above them. The ridgepole was splitting in two. It had a green–stick fracture.

The ridgepole of a traditional house in Jesús María is a long, strong tree trunk running from one end of the house to the other. It is of cedar if the house is properly made, of pine if the builder cut corners. My ridgepole was of pine. Termites had weakened it, the rain had saturated it, and it was simply giving up.

"Don't come in, Señora Cata. Don't come in," Don Paco yelled.

He ran for a *horcon*, the forked tree trunk a builder uses as a prop for a heavy beam. I ran for Rafael, the Cora who lived nearest me, and begged another horcon. Don Paco staggered in with one horcon and shoved it under the solid part of the ridgepole on one side of the split. Rafael struggled in with another horcon for the other side of the split. Both men tiptoed out.

I moved into my storeroom across the patio. Chela cleaned out another storeroom for Mike. The rain rained on, and the river kept rising.

On the eighth day, the river was one huge, boiling, crashing tor-rent, from the far side to halfway up the cliff to our ledge. It had swal-lowed the big guamuchil tree on the flats and was swamping Don Arnulfo's mango trees on the slope.

"It's drowning my little mangos," Doña Constancia cried as I passed their house.

Don Arnulfo's eldest son, the teacher, sat on his heels just above the orchard, silently watching as the trees swayed back and forth in the current, the brown water churning up to their middle branches. One lemon tree kept shaking back and forth violently, as if by a giant hand.

All along the lip of the ledge, people were watching the river, sit–

ting on walls, slouching against trees, squatting on their heels, all wet and all watching. Across the river, in front of every thatched hut, one or two white figures stood motionless. Whole trees came hurtling down the center of the river, their huge spreading roots bobbing grotesquely. Horcons that had supported beams came toppling down, end over end, in the current.

The innocents stayed in their dark, windowless room. In the patio, a hen stood in the rain, its legs tied together, its head hanging down, the picture of desolation. Three toads jumped onto the brick floor of my new kitchen.

My son Mike and I sloshed down to the bottom end of town to see how the Coras were faring. The houses were all still standing, but water was gushing out the windows of the new government building being constructed there and then rushing on, making a clean little cliff of sand. A dozen men in their big white hats and as many women in their black rebozos stood watching. Nobody said anything. The river was immense, ugly, dangerous. On the far side, it was crashing into breakers over an outcropping of rocks.

The church began filling up for early Mass the day the river burst its banks. By the time the water poured into and out of the government building, even the men were confessing and attending Mass daily.

Chela laughed.

"Jesús María is suddenly full of Catholics," she said.

In the daytime we scarcely heard the river, but at night it roared. It was an angry sound, dark and menacing. Over the roar, I could scarcely hear the whisper of the rain on the roof of my storeroom.

Then, as suddenly as it had started, the rain stopped. The river began to shrink. In just one day, it slid back from the mango trees and the government building, and patches of the flats began to emerge. All the soil had been washed away. Where Don Dionisio had planted his peanuts, there was now a sea of boulders. Don Pedro's stone wall had disappeared into a jumble of rocks.

The day after the rain stopped, I was able to wade to the bridge to cross the river and see a little girl with pneumonia. The sky was still overcast, the road up to El Cerro was still impassable, and no planes were flying in from Tepic. We were still marooned.

Finally, the day came when the sky was clear—"clean," they say in the Sierra. The stars were bright in the early morning, the road had dried enough for José to drive, and we were sure a plane would fly in. At last we could leave, we and the innocents. They had given up hope of finding the Huichols and were ready to return to Tepic and vegetables.

Mike and I shouldered our bags and, with our flashlights, picked our way to the bridge. The innocents, with their bare feet and their backpacks, came tramping after.

We sat in the back of the pickup on the way to the summit. It was bitterly cold. As the dawn began to break, the mountains began, little by little, to show their new colors. Green. Green. The male innocent sat with his long hair streaming behind him, smiling out over the green hills and the pinkening sky.

"Beautiful," he murmured. "Beautiful."

When I came back to the Sierra after a couple of weeks away, it was still as green as August, and flowers were blooming everywhere. Then, as "the dries" continued, the hills burned off, the plants shriveled in the sun, the flowers withered on their stems. The hills turned rosy gray, with only a green flash of cactus and mesquite to remind us of summertime.

After a couple of weeks, my roof was repaired. Pedro did it. I knew him well. He had built a little outdoor kitchen for me on the back of the house when I could no longer put up with the smoky kerosene stove. He assured me daily that I wasn't going to like it, that a kitchen should have walls. He was a very gloomy man.

In due course, the dry season came to an end, the rains started, the little plants sprang up, and tiny red velvet bugs scampered among them. The Sierra was green again.

Once more, however, it did rain during the dry season, the winter.

The rain started suddenly, without warning. It was a soft rain, a gentle rain, a rain that scarcely made a whisper on my new tile roof. It rained without stopping, all day and all night. It rained as if it would never stop.

In the morning, seventeen men turned out for early Mass.

13

Whom Does Not the Scorpion Sting?

I always knew that someday a scorpion would get me, but I wasn't thinking of scorpions when I put on my shoe.

Anyone living in the middle of the scorpion's own territory should know that scorpions like shoes. Anybody with any sense taps the shoes on the floor, toe up, before putting them on. I didn't. The agonizing stab of pain in my little toe remained to remind me of my folly for nearly twenty-four hours.

Short of death, there is nothing I can think of that is more leveling than a scorpion sting can be. I knew. I had had plenty of experience with scorpions stinging other people, and I knew their wicked ways. I had hoped that when a scorpion finally stung me I could be unflappable, meeting the situation with humor and aplomb. That is what I had hoped.

I had even figured out exactly what I was going to do. First, if the sting was on my hand, arm, foot, or leg, I was going to tie something tightly above the sting to keep the venom from circulating. Then I was going to inject hydrocortisone slowly into the vein on the back of my hand. After a few minutes, I would inject the antitoxin. (The cortisone would be to avoid a possible allergic reaction to the anti-toxin.) Then I was going to lie down and read a book.

Ha.

With the pain in my toe like that of a red-hot embroidery needle skewering into the bone, I pulled my carton of emergency medicines out from under my bed. After some fumbling, I found the fresh hy-podermic syringes and contrived to fill one with hydrocortisone.

Then I scrubbed the back of my left hand with alcohol. Now for the vein.

I pushed. I thrust. I jabbed. I tried again. And again. And again. I couldn't even break the skin.

I hobbled shoeless to the patio door.

I tried to call out cheerfully, but it sounded as if I might be whimpering. I cleared my throat.

"A scorpion stung me."

Chela and Don Paco were in Guadalajara on a buying trip. Arcelia's tall daughter Luz was in charge of the store. Providentially, she was crossing the patio from the storeroom with an armload of boxed store cookies. She heard me. She turned, aghast, then started to run.

She came back with Don Pedro. He was now working on the new Presidencia. His hands were dusty with cement. I didn't ask him to wash them. I just held out the fresh syringe I had filled from the one I had failed with.

"Where did it sting you?" he asked morosely, without taking the syringe. I told him.

"Why didn't you tie something above it?" he asked crossly. To Luz: "Get me a rag."

Eventually, he did wash his hands and gave me two shots in the conventional locations. He questioned me closely. Was my leg going numb? No. Was my throat closing up? No. Was I seeing double? No.

Satisfied, he left, saying gloomily as he ducked through the door, "It will probably stop hurting sometime tomorrow."

I lay down. I tried, as my mother had taught me when I was a child, to pretend it was the day after tomorrow. I failed. I forgot all about reading a book. Instead, I began thinking of some of the victims of scorpions I had taken care of.

There was Sofia, the dark, pretty mestiza girl who lived upriver, nearly at the head of The Street in Front of the Church. She was the first victim I had inoculated in her own home.

I found her lying on a cot in the bigger of the two rooms of the adobe house, a rag tied tightly at the base of her finger. Five girls were sitting around her, three on chairs, two on the cot. I recognized them all. They were girls who, like Sofia, went regularly to the curato to teach the little children their catechism. They were having an animated conversation about their own scorpion stings when I came in. I was appalled.

Sofia was obviously suffering, and here were all her friends, chattering as if it were a birthday party. It was against everything I had been taught or believed. A person ill or hurt ought to be given rest, quiet, and privacy.

"Shouldn't the girls perhaps go home?" I asked Sofia's mother as I filled the hypodermic syringe.

"I think Sofia perhaps likes to have her friends here," her mother said soothingly.

Sofia's sting was a sting like my own, with ceaseless, unremitting, unimaginable pain but no other symptoms. The scorpion's murderous little tail had stabbed Sofia in the finger when she opened the door.

There was a knock at my own door, the screened one into the patio, and Arcelia and Juana stooped in.

"A scorpion stung you," Arcelia said.

"Luz told us," Juana said. "She was scared."

"Is your throat closing up?" Arcelia asked me anxiously.

"No," I said. "It's just my toe."

"So you're not seeing double, then?" Arcelia sounded relieved.

"It's a good thing Chela isn't here," Juana said. "She'd be having hysterics."

Arcelia and Juana both laughed and laughed. My toe was killing me.

"You can be glad your sting is the kind that hurts," Juana said consolingly. "When your throat closes up, it's dreadful. Do you remember, Arcelia, the time Chela got stung in the vein?"

As I lay there with my toe screaming, Arcelia and Juana talked. They talked about all the times Chela had been stung because their father insisted that she wash off the cement counter in the kitchen in the dark of the morning and she always wiped it with the flat of her hand. There was often a scorpion there. They talked about their own scorpion stings and their children's. My toe screamed on and on. They talked about the hens that got stung.

"As long as they can still stand up, they have a chance," Juana explained to me. "But when they fall over, you know that they will never stand up again."

Finally, after what seemed like a couple of hours, the two women rose to go.

"We'll tell Inez you got stung," Juana said as she sloped through the door.

I thought I would be glad to have them gone, my toe hurt me so. To my amazement, though, after they left it hurt a great deal more. I would have liked to call them back. Instead, I tried to remember, as Juana had said, that I should be glad that it was the kind that hurt. I remembered all too well some of the other kinds.

There was the sting that rendered the poor victim desperate, throwing his arms and legs around, wanting to sit up one moment and to lie down the next, and needing help to do either. There was a treatment for that beyond the shots: a bath in a washtub filled with tepid water into which one had thrown a handful of salt and a handful of lime, a bath repeated three times over with a writhing, thrashing child. Numbness all over went with that sting, blurred vision that eventually cleared to double vision, a struggle to breathe. If I had had that kind of sting, I would be having even less success in remaining unflappable than I was having now.

Babies had died of scorpion stings on the trails from the ranchos to Jesús María. That handsome little arachnid with the claws on its pincers really did have death in its tail. Sometimes older children died, too, and old people if they were weak. Sometimes there were miracles.

I remembered how Martin had come to my window at four in the morning with Rosario in his arms. Rosario was three years old, a beautiful little lump of a girl with a smiling mouth and black, almond eyes. She was absolutely inert, unconscious, and scarcely breathing at all.

(The pain in my toe was intolerable. Why didn't Inez come to see me? Juana had said she would tell her.)

Rosario had met up with her scorpion at ten o'clock at night, six hours before her father brought her to me. Martin's mother was a *curandera* and had spent the night singing and sucking and blowing smoke from her slender, elegant pipe, but to no avail. Martin had finally taken matters into his own hands and had carried Rosario in from his *ranchito*, an hour and a half away.

Luckily, I was wearing a short nightgown. I pulled a wraparound skirt over it and grabbed a shirt, which I buttoned on the way to the curato. The stars were so bright we needed no flashlights. In the little clinic, I lighted the kerosene lamp, Martin placed Rosario gently on the splintery table, and I began filling the syringe. Martin tenderly unfolded the black rebozo Rosario was wrapped in.

Rosa came at the first light and, with her, her mother–in–law, Martin's curandera mother, Apolinaria. Rosa brought tortillas. Apolinaria brought an offering. It was inside a snowy white cotton cloth. Apolinaria lifted back the points of the cloth, and there was one of the little white disks I had so often seen a Cora lay reverently at the feet of one of the santitos in the church. I had never seen one so close. It was of white native cotton swirled into an exquisite little disk, absolutely round, no bigger than the palm of a child's hand. It lay on the cloth like a jewel.

I had seen Coras offering their prayer disks to one saint or another in the church almost daily since I had been in Jesús María, but never before had a Cora prayed into one with me present. It was an awesome experience.

First, Apolinaria took a gigantic breath of air all the way down to her pelvis. Then she bowed her head over the disk, which was lying on her hand on the open white cloth, and began to speak into it, softly, paying out as little breath as possible, on and on and on, without taking another breath until I was almost drowning, as one does watching for someone to come up from underwater who stays and stays in order to frighten his mother, or sister, or wife. When she came to the end of her apparently inexhaustible wind, she took another enormous breath, and I, too, could breathe again.

Apolinaria continued to pray for three or four more breaths. Then Rosa prayed. Then Martin. Then Apolinaria folded the corners of the white cloth over the little disk, now full of prayers for Rosario, and Rosa took the cloth package from Apolinaria and slipped out through the big wooden doors.

I knew, because I had seen so many times, what Rosa would do in church. First, she would sink on her knees and bless herself in the complicated Indian way. Then she would pray for a few minutes before rising and going to the chosen santito. She would carefully take the disk out of its cloth wrapping and hold it high, where the santito could not fail to see it. Then she would lay it gently at the feet of the statue before kneeling again in the main aisle of the church and leaving.

By the time Rosa came back to the curato, I had given Rosario two more shots. She was still so numb she didn't feel them. She was breathing stertorously, and her little heart was racing.

Apolinaria slipped out; Martin, Rosa, and I stayed on, numb ourselves with anxiety. Rosa and Martin sat on the table on either side of Rosario, one or the other patting her rhythmically. I sat on the homemade wooden chair that always threatened to collapse.

"Where did Apolinaria go?" I asked.

"To make some white atole," Rosa said.

I didn't know what that was. I had often had atole, a drink like liquid cornstarch pudding, vanilla, chocolate, or strawberry, but white atole?

"It's just made of tortilla dough. No sugar," Rosa said kindly. "Sometimes people can drink it when they can't drink anything else."

A drink made of tortilla dough?

"But where can she make atole?"

The ranchito was miles away.

"Someplace," Martin said. "Someplace where there's a fire in the stove."

Finally, Apolinaria did come back. She had a white enamel mug, almost full of milky white gruel. Rosa stood up. She supported Rosario's little head while Apolinaria tried to pour the white atole into Rosario's mouth. Rosario now had strength enough to spit out the atole. It ran down her chin. Rosa wiped Rosario's chin with her rebozo and put the child's head down again.

Rosario could move a little now, but her heart was still racing. I looked at my watch. It was nine o'clock, and Don Serafim would be in the Health Center.

I stumbled over and begged his help.

"What can I do for that little heart?" I asked him.

"How much does Rosario weigh by now, do you suppose?" he asked as he clumped into the medicine closet.

Half an hour after the shot of Don Serafim's medicine, Rosario's heart slowed down. She opened her eyes and looked around and then closed them again quickly. She was seeing double. She gave a hoarse little cry, and Martin took her in his arms.

It was two o'clock in the afternoon before Rosario recovered enough to drink some white atole, and four before she nibbled a cookie and I dismissed her. Martin, Rosa, Apolinaria, and I all con‐gratulated ourselves: Rosa for making tortillas before sunup (we had never eaten them), Apolinaria for the offering to the santito and the white atole, Martin for bringing Rosario to me, and I for having a friend in Don Serafim. We had all been afraid that Rosario would die.

Somebody was at my door.

"Come in, come in," I called. In spite of my best efforts, I sounded pitiful. My toe hurt furiously.

"I made you some white atole," Inez said. "Sometimes people can drink it when they can't drink anything else."

So Inez *had* come. So Juana and Arcelia *had* told her.

I nudged myself into a sitting position and took the cup. The white atole was horrible, but I drank it, every drop. Meanwhile, Inez talked.

Inez was the oldest sister. She seldom ventured out of her house except to visit the Virgin and attend Mass. I was amazed and touched that she would come to see me. Her husband was living with another woman in Tepic, her son was married and living in Colorado, and she lived alone with her daughter, the other Luz. She was a soft, genial woman with a full, unwrinkled face, apparently untouched by her losses.

"It's a good thing Chela isn't here," she said, laughing. "She'd be having hysterics." She sobered. "It's a good thing it's the kind that hurts. There are other kinds that are worse."

"I know," I said. "I've seen some bad cases."

"Did Chela ever tell you about the time the scorpion stung her in the vein?"

"No," I said. "Please tell me all about it."

Inez did. Then she told me about her own scorpion stings, about

Luz's, and about how her favorite little calf had been stung and recovered and how her billy goat had been stung and died. She told me
that I should always be extra careful after a rain, even if it comes in
the dry season when the scorpions are under the rocks. A scorpion
thinks it's summer, she told me, that it's going to keep on being wet.
So it looks for a tree with bark it can hide under, but there aren't
many trees right here so the scorpion goes into a house instead.

And into a shoe, I thought.

"Have you ever seen a hen that has been stung by a scorpion?"
she asked me.

"No," I said. "But I understand that if one falls down, it will never
stand up again."

I succeeded in keeping Inez with me for over an hour. Then she
rose and said she must go to the Rosary.

As she ducked out through the door, I heard myself calling after
her. From the tone of my voice, I didn't sound the least bit unflappable. In it, there was nothing of humor or aplomb. In a few short
hours, I had ceased to be a spectator and had become a member of
the cast.

"Please," I called after Inez. "Please come back and tell Juana and
Arcelia. It hurts more when I'm alone—and bring me some more
white atole."

14

At 3:00 P.M. They Kill Him

*I*t was the Wednesday before Easter when I got back to Jesús María after my monthly week in Guadalajara. I was fantastically lucky in getting a ride in the mission plane. On Tuesday there had been no room for me on the commercial plane. It had flown out twice, full of tourists and Coras going home from picking chile peppers on the coast. There would be no flight on Thursday. The Coras would not permit it. Padre Jacinto was flying a couple of seminary students out on Wednesday, and the bishop, on his way to Guadalajara, said I might go along. I sat on an oil can, and the students sat on the floor.

In Jesús María, the tourists were highly visible.

An earnest young woman with mousy hair was sitting on the ground with her back against the outside of the atrium wall, scribbling purposefully in her notebook. She was obviously an anthropologist. I hoped the Coras would not give her a hard time.

An angry–looking couple, both with long tangled hair, were tramping up The Street in Front of the Church arguing noisily in French.

Two bearded youths from the States stopped me to ask where they could buy peyote. "That's the Huichols," I told them. "You've come to the wrong place."

A tall young lady in a long dress of pink cotton sidled across the road to avoid a litter of baby pigs. She looked terribly alone.

When I got home, I found two strange women in my house, in the room with no window and the door onto the street. Before I had recovered from my outrage, Chela breezed in from the patio.

"I rented one of your rooms," she announced cheerfully. "I knew you wouldn't mind." She smiled affectionately. "I left you your bed."

It was about all she had left me. The lady tourists, one a Mexican journalist from Mexico City and the other a gift-shop owner from Albuquerque, New Mexico, had one of my tables and my two indoor chairs. They also had a beach chair that opened out to sleep on and the cot that had thrown me the first night I was in the house.

I looked over the situation, did my best to be gracious, failed, and left.

In the patio were more tourists. Chela had apparently rented every bed she could improvise in the string of rooms and storerooms along the far side of the patio. As I passed through, Chela introduced me to an amiable museum director from Mexico City with his Chilean wife, a couple of stiff Swiss gentlemen with the most elaborate cameras I had ever seen, an ever-smiling Japanese who proved to be a linguist, and a solitary Italian girl in tight black pants. They all seemed to have nothing in common but misery. The heat was suffocating. Chela had appropriated the chair and table from my outdoor kitchen to add to her own, and the guests sat together drinking Coca-Cola and wishing, I suspected, that it was beer.

The one happy note was the music of a reed flute, sweet and melancholy, floating in on the heavy air like a silken thread.

Chela's little nephew, Filemon's older brother Panchillo, kicked the lop-eared burro through the gate to dump a load of firewood on a big pile beside the kitchen door. All the tubs were brimming with water. Chela apologized.

"Nobody can work on Holy Thursday or Good Friday," she said. "We have to get everything done today."

Then she remembered.

"This is the last day you can go to the river, too, if you want to take a bath or wash clothes."

The Swiss gentlemen looked affronted.

"And you know that, after today, we can't turn on a radio or a tape recorder, or play any kind of music, or ride in a truck or on a mule or even a burro," she said.

The museum director smiled.

"We know," he said gently. "We've read a book."

I observed the courtesies and escaped to say hello to Don Paco. He was presiding in the store. There was plenty of custom.

Padre Domingo was plodding down The Street in Front of the Church, his brown shirt sticking to his back, his grubby white pants flapping around his knees.

"You're just in time," he said sociably. "The governor's grand-daughter has the itch."

Don Nicomedes was staying in town all the time now, as a governor should. I wanted very much to see him. He had promised to ask permission for me to take pictures. On this occasion, he couldn't give it himself. I was glad to go with the padre.

The little girl clearly had impetigo. From his woven Cora bag, the padre pulled aspirin, his ugly black salve, Coca-Cola, and the inevitable penicillin, which he shot into the rump of the screaming child.

I asked about the photographs.

"No," Don Nicomedes said. "Nobody can take photographs. Nobody."

I thought of the stiff Swiss gentlemen. The governor read my mind.

"And I'm afraid that anybody who tries will lose his camera," he said.

The padre hugged the little girl, rocked her, and sang to her until she stopped crying, then put her down and we started back to the curato. On the way, we met a merry group of Coras sweeping the street. The padre said something to them in Cora, and they all laughed.

"The Judios come this way," the padre said.

The Judios, I knew, were the three hundred or more young men from all over the mountains who were going to paint their bodies, put on animal masks, and terrorize the town during the last days of Holy Week.

"Why do people keep calling them the Judios?" I protested. "The Jews. The Jesuits didn't know any better with their medieval Catholicism, but this is the twentieth century, padre. Can't we call them something else now?"

Padre Domingo laughed.

"The Coras have no idea that the Jews were ever a people," he said, "less still that they are a people now. Ask any old Cora. He'll tell you the Judios represent the devils as they used to be long, long ago. Their name is only a name now, nothing more."

The Judios didn't take over the town until Thursday, but the museum director and I got a sneak preview Wednesday night. We stumbled up the lava flow to the mesa of San Miguel in the dark. There was a moon, but it was misted over. In front of the Casa Fuerte, the council house, the Judios were shuffling back and forth, sometimes jogging a little, a throng of them. In the darkness, we could faintly see white paint on almost naked bodies, big white animal masks, a few white plumes. Something at their painted waists (I later discovered they were box-turtle shells with pebbles inside) jangled with every step.

Two of the boys were dancing with their arms around each other, clowning. They stopped in front of me, pushed up their masks, and demanded cigarettes. When they saw I had a pack, bought for the occasion, they demanded them all. I gave each of them two. They laughed and shuffled away.

While we were watching, the mist cleared away. Even with the bright light of the moon, the stars, a million of them, stabbed through the blackness of the sky. The museum director and I picked our way down without turning on our flashlights.

In the middle of the night, the cot on which the lady journalist was sleeping created a diversion. It threw her just as it had thrown me, except that it threw her against the wall. It took time to extricate her. In the morning, Chela brought her two planks and four oil cans to make a more stable bed.

The fiesta began in earnest that morning, Thursday. Fray Nicolas paced back and forth on the roof of the church, swinging the wooden clacker to call the Coras to their special Mass. The church bells were stilled.

I had slipped into the church the day before and had found it completely changed.

Purple hangings concealed the santitos up the wall behind the altar. Purple curtains concealed the santitos on the platforms before the windows on both sides of the nave. The big Christ with the exposed bones was shrouded in a white sheet.

In front of the altar had been the Nazarene, the tragic primitive figure of Christ reviled. His bowed head was crowned with a fillet of woven palm, his robe a rough purple shift. He stooped under the weight of a heavy wooden cross that leaned against his left shoulder. Tied to his right hand was a sheaf of grass, his scepter. Dripping from his neck was a long string of tassels, flowers from the tree the Coras call *clavellina*.

This Thursday morning he had disappeared. I asked Padre Domingo where the Coras had put him.

"In jail," he said shortly. Jail, I discovered, was the baptismal room opposite the Christ with exposed bones.

In place of the Nazarene, there was a black blanket on the floor in front of the altar, and on the blanket lay an exquisite little statue of Christ, an almost black statue I had never seen before.

Don Nazario, tall, slender, old, his chiseled face absolutely expressionless as usual, stood with his back against the side wall, his arms folded on his chest.

Suddenly, along the side of the mountain behind Jesús María, on the trail that slanted from the mesa of San Miguel down to the town, here came the Judios. I could see them out of the big doors of the church. They came running in lockstep, their wooden swords uplifted in front of them, a formidable flying frieze of black-and-white bodies and big white masks.

I stepped outside. More Judios were approaching on The Street Behind the Church. I could hear the thud of their feet hitting the road and could faintly hear the jangle of their turtle shells.

By the time the church had filled with Coras and the Mass had started, the Judios had poured into the town and were running, dancing, and committing obscenities in the street. The tourists had poured out of their hidey-holes and were watching, enthralled.

Back in the church, the Cora orchestra was playing in the organ loft: three violins, a triangle, and a drum. The music was discordant but strangely moving.

The Authorities—Don Nicomedes, his second in command, the judge, and the Cora police—were sitting on a bench up front, along the side wall facing the altar. They were holding in front of them their symbols of office, the slender batons of red Brazil wood with ribbons hanging from their tips. The color of the ribbons proclaimed the rank of the Authority. Don Nicomedes's ribbons were white, as befitted the governor.

Padre Domingo celebrated the Mass. The Authorities then solemnly laid their rods of power, their symbols of office, on the altar. They were relinquishing their command to the painted youths clowning outside. The music stopped.

I followed the Authorities as they filed out of the church. Across the street, below the porch of the old Presidencia, was a white horse, its saddle covered with a white blanket. But riding was prohibited today, wasn't it? I ran to catch up with Don Nicomedes.

"Whose horse is that?" I asked him.

"The White Centurion's," Don Nicomedes answered. "You'll see."

The Judios had all gathered in the parade ground of the Moors. To watch them, I joined the tourists.

The masks were marvelous. I had seen several of them before. Several of the youths in town had given me secret viewings as they were happily molding their own out of pieces of paper carton and corn-flour paste. One I recognized instantly. It had the snout of a pig, teeth cut from a sardine can, real deer antlers, and a head of the coarse white hair that springs from one of Mexico's weirder cacti. Its owner had been making it under a kareton across the river where I had gone to take a blood sample of his little niece. He saw me looking at him now and stopped jogging to come, holding out his hand to shake mine. His black soot came off on my hand.

"Oh," he said. "Pardon."

Most of the Judios were not so courtly. They ran crouched over like apes. They made animal sounds of grunts and coos. They invented comedies. They pretended to grow angry at one another and fenced with their wooden swords. They imitated animals coupling. They jogged, and danced, and clowned, and occasionally darted forth to threaten spectators who came too close. The spectators screamed with delight and ran.

Seen up close, the Judios' body paint was a work of pure art. It was in bold, original designs of black and white stripes, whorls, and geometrics, the same on the left side as on the right. The masks were magnificent, grotesques of every kind of imaginary animal. Only the novices were less than spectacular. The novices were painted all black and wore small white hats with little plumes. The captains wore black shirts, white Cora pants, and peaked hats with white plumes that curved up and forward over their noses.

Throughout the remaining days of Holy Week, the tourists remained in the streets, captivated by the Judios' antics. Only the museum director perceived the whole drama for what it was to the Coras: the conflict between Good and Evil acted out from a script the Jesuits had written for them some three hundred years ago. As is so often the case, Evil was more fun, and the tourists almost never set foot in the church.

There the air was heavy with the sweet, smoky fragrance of the incense, incense from the gum of the silvery *copal* tree. Two Cora women were sitting on the floor, their full skirts spread out around them. From time to time, they pinched more incense into their crude clay bowls. Between them, on a black blanket, lay the small dark Christ on his dark wooden cross. On the floor around the blanket glimmered tall candles in the Coras' handsome old brass candlesticks.

Between the blanket and the altar, as if guarding the dark little Christ, two young Coras stood, their feet apart, their hands clasped behind their backs.

Fray Nicolas had pushed all the pews back against the side walls. When I slipped into the church, the Cora orchestra was playing gloriously in the choir loft, and a throng of Coras, families of them, stood facing the little Christ there on the black blanket. Slowly, one family after another advanced to kneel and pray. Then each one—father, mother, and each of the children—bent down to kiss the wounds of Christ before rising and leaving the church, heads up, eyes straight ahead, faces expressionless.

Don Nazario continued to stand in his accustomed place against the wall, his arms folded on his chest.

In the church that Thursday morning, there started a ritual that lasted into the night and after.

Back from the little Christ on the black blanket, there were always two small boys kneeling on a carpet of banana leaves. On their heads they had chaplets of orange leaves. In their hands they held lighted candles. They knelt there motionless, their eyes straight ahead, until an older Cora, from behind the purple curtain on the left side of the nave, brought two other little boys to take their places. The previous two retired with dignity behind the purple drapery. They were the Apostles.

Back nearer the door were the Pharisees, four young Coras as straight as arrows, standing to form four corners of a square. They were all in white, their white hats on the floor at their feet. Each had a lance in his hand, which he pounded on the floor from time to time. At regular intervals, the White Centurion, splendid in his white apparel and red neckerchief, would march four replacements into the church. As the original Pharisees picked up their hats and marched out, the new Pharisees would put their hats on the floor and themselves stand in formation, from time to time pounding the floor with their lances.

Two Pharisees guarded the door outside. The Judios, like most of the tourists, never set foot in the church.

On leaving the church, I checked into Padre Domingo's clinic. In spite of all the Coras who had thronged into town, there were relatively few patients. The season for respiratory infections was past, and it wasn't yet time for dysentery. As I left the curato through the burros' entrance, another family of Coras was entering the church to kiss the wounds of Christ.

Back at the house, the gift-shop owner from Albuquerque was waiting for me.

"There's only one toilet for all of us," she told me, consternation in her light blue eyes.

"There are only six toilets in Jesús María," I told her.

"And we have to flush it with a bucket of water from one of those tubs in the patio."

"Isn't it lucky we have so much water," I said heartlessly before I left.

I ate in the curato. I was too tired to deal with the tourists at Chela's. Chuy served me herself, grinning a little.

Things were happening in the town. When I trudged back to Chela's after lunch, the Coras were feasting in front of the Health Center. Women were sitting on the ground surrounded by big clay cauldrons from which they were dipping out atole and serving rice and roasted squash. The Judios had disappeared.

At Chela's, I found my two housemates happily occupied. The lady journalist was busily noting down all the extraordinary things the Judios had done that morning. The gift–shop owner was pricing her purchases before she forgot. She had a handsome collection of hand–woven Cora bags. One could not but concede that she had educated taste.

I felicitated both of them and went to sleep.

It was getting dark when I woke up. I took my flashlight and started back to the church. Most of the tourists elected to stay at Chela's, having heard that the evening provided only "something like Stations of the Cross." The museum director had read a book. He accompanied me.

As we approached the church, we could see that the Judios were swarming there, on the street and up on the wall of the atrium, all the way around, a solid line of them crouching, posturing, threatening. Running toward us were four fearsome–looking Judios with their swords outstretched. Two of them crossed their swords behind the back of the museum director, two behind me. They pushed us, stumbling, into the atrium. Two Judios guarding the gate lifted their swords to let us through.

The atrium was crowded with Coras. Some of them were sitting on the ground around small fires. Some were churning around. Several children were sleeping on blankets.

Suddenly, all were on their feet. The "something like Stations of the Cross" was about to happen.

The Nazarene was there, in front of the church, surrounded by Pharisees who were clattering their lances together over his head, a chilling sound. A Cora in a white robe with a crown of woven palm was there in front of the Nazarene, obviously meant to represent Christ. Beside him was a young boy, similarly dressed and bound with a rope. The Black Centurion on his black horse appeared from nowhere, took the rope, and led the Christs, the Nazarene, the Pharisees, and the waiting Coras in a long procession out through the gate and onto The Street in Front of the Church.

The Judios in the street, a horde of them, formed themselves into solid ranks along both sides of the procession.

"Nobody's going to get out of that little walk," the museum director murmured as we sat down on the long log against the front of the church.

Nobody could get out of the atrium, either. The few of us left had to stay. The Judios on the wall and at the gate saw to that.

Friday morning there was no Mass. The Judios ran down from San Miguel as they had on Thursday, but today they were in full glowing color. In place of black and white, they had painted themselves in bold designs of black with hot pink, lavender, red, turquoise blue, lemon yellow. Their new masks were colored to match their body paint. They were grotesquely gorgeous.

The church had changed, too. The dark little Christ was no longer on the floor but high up behind the new altar. On the old altar behind it were santitos, two saints I didn't know, and a small mourning Virgin, along with seven tall candles in the Coras' brass candlesticks.

Don Nazario was sitting in a pew at the side of the nave, asleep.

I slipped out of the church and sauntered down to join the tourists and the local mestizos, who were watching the Judios as they jogged, and clowned, and pretended to fight. It was terribly hot. I started back to Padre Domingo's clinic.

In front of the old Presidencia there was now a black horse, its black saddle blanket decorated with red roses. Beside him was the Black Centurion. He was dressed all in black—black suit, black hat, black boots—with a bright red sash from his right shoulder to his left hip. He had a long black lance in his hand and cruel spurs at his heels. He looked indescribably sinister. As I got to the gate of the atrium, he suddenly leapt on his horse, spurred it, and tore past me at breakneck speed. There was something plastered against the tip of his lance.

Padre Domingo came plodding across the street from the Presidencia.

"What was that he had on his lance?" I asked the padre.

"The sentence. I had to write it for them," he said, indicating the Coras on the porch of the Presidencia. "None of them could."

I looked. Not one of the educated Coras was there, not one of the young teachers, not Don Arnulfo or the principal of the school. The bishop had told me sadly that the young teachers were ashamed of the costumbre. And the rumor was that Don Arnulfo and the school principal were "Halleluyas," converts to an enthusiastic evangelical sect. Only the true-blue-Cora Coras were on the porch today.

I was cross with myself. Watching the Judios had been so entertaining, I had missed a crucial event in the Easter drama.

The big event of the morning was the pursuit of the big and little Cora Christs in their white shifts and crowns of palm. They came out of the atrium running, hand in hand. The whole army of Judios pounded after them. Somewhere along the route, the pursued slipped into a house, but the pursuers kept pursuing, running at full, pounding, jangling speed, their black and pink and yellow paint glowing in the sun, their swords uplifted, some of them clutching their masks with their left hands to keep them on their heads. They ran and ran in what turned into a gigantic circle around dozens and dozens of houses. They were like a huge multicolored serpent chasing its own tail.

At high noon came the one religious observance in which the Coras and the mestizos joined. It was the meeting between the Nazarene and his mother, under the ramada in front of the Health Center.

The men went first, down The Street in Front of the Church, led by the Black Centurion with the sentence still on the tip of his lance. He looked even more sinister than before. After him came the Pharisees, now in dark blue shirts. Then followed the Nazarene in his purple robe and crown of palm, his cross supported behind by a stalwart Cora. Then came Padre Domingo and the rest of the men. A brigade of Judios surrounded them, half of the painted ones closing in along one side of the procession, the other half closing in along the other side, their swords at the ready to foil escape.

I went with the women. Four boys carried the litter of a big, mourning Virgin with her purple robe and crown of stars. We women followed, suffering. The sun was savage. Another brigade of Judios crowded us in on both sides, all of us in intimate contact with other hot female bodies, fore, aft, and sideways. A tone-deaf mestiza led the other non-Cora women in a dreary church song. We reached the ramada steaming.

Padre Domingo, in the shade of the ramada, delivered a long, passionate sermon. We sinners, trapped by the Judios who circled around us, simmered in the sun. I saw the museum director standing among the men. He was wiping the back of his neck with a handkerchief.

All things come to an end, and so, mercifully, did Padre Domingo's sermon. Nobody fainted on the way back to the church, and, somehow, I made it on to Chela's for lunch. The Coras were eating theirs again. It was fish today with nopales, the edible cactus, and bananas smeared with honey.

Nobody wanted to go to The Seven Last Words of Christ with me, so I went alone. The church was nearly empty. Only a few mestizos sat on the benches pushed against the wall. The only Cora present was Don Nazario, who had lighted the seven tall candles on the old altar and who extinguished them, one by one, as Fray Nicolas read the seven Bible verses and delivered a brief homily on each. Toward the end he hurried a little, looking from time to time at his watch. He had barely finished when the Black Centurion and the eight Pharisees erupted into the church, tramped down to the altar, lifted their long lances together, and speared the little Christ up above, the dark little Christ on the dark wooden cross.

It was exactly three o'clock.

The men had their hats on, low over their brows. They had red kerchiefs tied over their mouths and noses, like bandits. As they noisily shuffled back to the door, they thumped their lances on the floor. The Black Centurion's spurs clanged on the tiles.

The mestizos all left the church. I, a trifle shaken, stayed on.

From one of the bell towers there floated down one long, sorrowful note from a Cora flute.

Two Cora youths brought in a litter and set it down near the altar. Two others brought in a wire cage, shaped like half a barrel, covered with colored ribbons and paper flowers.

It was now the time to bring forth the most beloved of all the santitos, the Santo Enterro, Christ in the tomb. All the year he lay hidden in a dark casket to which the Coras took their offerings and their most ardent prayers. Now, on the day of the crucifixion, he was to emerge for a few precious hours so his people could adore him.

Two elderly Coras, obviously the santito's caretakers, enlisted the help of two younger, stronger Coras to lift the casket out of the window niche and onto the floor. There, one of the caretakers reverently removed the lid of the coffin. The other tenderly lifted out the little image, protected from his hands by a black cloth. It was ancient, primitive, exquisite. It appeared to be made of wax, with its hair and beard painted on. There was a wig to put on it, then a crown, before it was laid reverently on the litter. Four men put on the beflowered cage and fastened it down. Then the elderly caretakers accompanied the youths as they carried the litter out of the church. I followed.

The street still had its tourists. The girl with the long pink cotton dress had taken up with the bearded boys from the States. They all seemed to be getting along nicely without peyote.

The angry couple were still arguing in French, but they had combed their hair.

The mousy girl was still sitting on the ground with her back against the wall, but the Judios had confiscated her notebook.

They were shuffling back and forth now in front of the ramada. They had had a hard day and were tired.

Back in Chela's patio, the Swiss gentlemen were sitting, looking glum. The Judios had taken their cameras away from them when they tried to take pictures surreptitiously, and they were both indignant and afraid they had lost their cameras for good. They had a special plane coming for them the next day.

The rest were staying on.

The gift–shop owner had no intention of leaving until she had bought masks. The lady journalist wanted to be able to write a *complete* story. The Japanese linguist, who, it turned out, spoke Italian among the seven languages in which he was fluent, was endeavoring, with a lot of toothy laughter, to teach Japanese to the Italian girl in the tight black pants. The amiable museum director and his wife remained friendly and bland.

That evening, the Coras took the little Christ back to the church. I went with Chela to see. He lay in his beflowered cage while Coras, old and young, and Chela, too, cried and cried around him.

Finally, the two old men prepared him once more for the tomb. Still crying, they held him upright over the floor to remove his crown, five long, jeweled pins. Lovingly, they lifted off his wig to reveal the ancient painted head. At last, he was once more in his aged casket and once more in his niche in the wall.

Chela and I escaped before the procession. The Judios were already gathering, and some were starting to climb up on the wall.

The next morning, Saturday, the second time the clacker sounded, we all straggled over to the atrium, all except for the Swiss gentlemen, who stiffly bid us good-bye. They were sitting in the patio with their accoutrements around them: backpacks, sleeping bags, a tent rolled up in a professional way, a complete field kitchen. The Coras had returned their cameras on their promise not to use them again.

I took my own camera to the atrium with me. Several of the young men behind masks had asked me to take pictures of them. I had no permission, I told them. That's only Thursdays and Fridays, they told me. Saturday you can take all you like. I didn't want to get knocked down again, but I did take my camera.

Chela's guests arranged themselves on the covered porch of the curato. I sat down on the log against the front of the church to wait.

The Authorities and a good showing of Cora families sedately arrived and sedately entered the church. The Judios, now with their paint smeared and ugly, swarmed into the atrium. The captains, their peaked hats and long plumes magenta now, lay prone in front of the church door. The rest of the Judios lay on their stomachs, side by side, in two facing columns from the gate of the atrium to the door of the church.

The clacker sounded a third time as a Cora paced with it on the roof of the church, and one could faintly hear, from inside the church, Padre Domingo intoning the admonition to examine one's conscience, the beginning of the Mass. This, however, was not a Mass. It was a special service for the Coras, which ended with the Gloria when the silent world exploded in sound. The bell beside the altar pealed out. The Coras in the towers swung the three great bells: BONG BONG BENG BONG BONG. Rockets hissed in the atrium and thundered in the sky. Bedlam broke loose.

The Judios leapt up to perform a comedy of terror. They darted, crouching, one way and another, as if looking for escape. With every rocket, seven or eight of them would leap into the air and fall dead, only to rise again. Five fell on top of one another. Two fell in my lap, smudging my dress. Finally, one corpse did not rise. Friends sur-rounded him, nattering and cooing, striking poses of horror and grief. Four of them ran out of the atrium and returned with a short ladder on which they placed their fallen comrade to run with him out of the gate and to join the rest of the Judios running, running down The Street in Front of the Church to the bottom end of town.

This was the end of the Judios in the Coras' Easter pageant. In the drama the Jesuits had taught them some three hundred years ago, Good had now triumphed. Evil was on its way to wash off its paint in the river.

I stayed in the atrium long enough to watch the Authorities leave the church. They marched out solemnly, in single file, Don Nic-omedes in the lead. Each had his baton, his rod of power, held out in front of him, its ribbons dangling from the tip. Once more we had a government of comparative justice and complete decorum.

The tourists ran with the Judios down to the river. The gift-shop lady bought so many masks the other guests had to help her carry them back to my house. She packed them in gunnysacks for which Chela charged her only a little more than they were worth. When José came for the Swiss gentlemen, she went along, a traveling em-porium, hoping to find better ways of packing things in Tepic.

Don Paco's tape recorder started blasting out Mexican country music in the store. I fiddled with my radio, trying to get some news from Tepic. Cocks began to crow and dogs to bark. Three mestizos rode by on very fine mules, obviously happy to be in the saddle again.

In the afternoon I took the lady journalist, the Chilean lady, and the Italian girl up the river to my hidden pool. They were glad to get clean. I didn't tell them about the leeches.

It had been a tiring day. The tourists went to bed early. Don Paco put on his best embroidered shirt and escorted Chela and me to mid-night Mass. The pews were again arranged crosswise. The church was full, but only with mestizos. Not a single Cora was there, not even Don Nazario.

When the Mass was over and we trickled out into the atrium, we found Coras there. For them, Holy Week was still going on. They were tying cornstalks and banana leaves to stakes driven into the ground, to line an avenue from the church out through the gate and away up The Street in Front of the Church. No Cora spoke to us as we passed by.

In the morning, I saw what the avenue was for. When I got to The Street in Front of the Church, there was music in the atrium from two sets of musicians: the orchestra that had played in the choir loft and the drummers and piper who had escorted the Moors. Both groups were playing their hearts out, different music but at the same time. The atrium was filled with Coras, laughing and chattering.

Down the avenue, which ran up the street as far as I could see, came the Authorities, walking slowly in two files with a space between them. Behind them, three Cora women were bearing a litter with the small mourning Virgin on it, the one that had been on the old altar. Two young Coras had another santito on a litter that they were tilting in front of the Virgin so the santito appeared to be bowing to her. The Virgin's litter was tilting as she bowed back. As the two young Coras turned to run back to the church, laughing, two other young men came running out of the church with another santito. Meeting, the two santitos bowed to each other. Then the second two young men ran with their santito into the church, while the first two ran back with theirs to bow again to the Virgin. The running back and forth went on and on.

An elderly Cora turned to me, smiling.

"They're telling her," he said, over the discord of the musicians, "that Christ is risen."

Finally, the Authorities arrived and entered the church, now with its purple hangings torn down. Padre Domingo helped the young Coras put the Virgin and the other santitos in a row in front of the new altar. They now allowed him to touch them. Family by family, the Coras straggled out of the atrium. Those who had come from other parts of the mountains said good-bye and went to hunt their mules. The Judios, now amiable young men with clean, bright shirts of sea green, salmon pink, rosy orange, blue violet, and American Beauty red, with shiny black hair and shiny clean faces, were looking for a place to sleep some more before starting home. Jesús María was Jesús María again. It would be another year before it would once more be Jerusalem of 33 A.D.

After Chela's tourists had all taken their leave, I had a chance to ask Padre Domingo about things that had perplexed me. I was holding a little girl's leg out straight so he could bandage her knee.

"How on earth did they know?" I asked him. "The Judios were pure Coras, but the Centurions and the Pharisees—how did the Coras know that the Bible says it was the Romans who killed Christ?"

"The Jesuits were good teachers," Padre Domingo the Franciscan said dryly.

"And the timing—they came into the church at exactly three o'clock. They never had watches until recently."

"They had the sun," Padre Domingo said.

"And the santitos who ran out on Sunday to bow to the Virgin and each other—who were they?"

Padre Domingo stopped bandaging and looked at me unbelievingly.

"They were John the Beloved and Christ resuscitated. Catareen," he said, lapsing into English, "haven't you learned anything yet?"

15

Almost as Glorious as a Wedding

In May, the only bearable time of the day was the very early morning. I would get up when it was still dark to start a fire in my stove. Even so early, the air was thick with heat. The world was drying up from the long, dry winter.

One morning, as I sleepily emerged from my house, I could see that there was someone down at the far end of the patio. It was Don Paco. He called to me softly so as not to awaken Chela.

"Señora Cata," he called. "A goat died this morning."

"What of?" I called.

I could barely see Don Paco, it was still so dark. I stumbled down the long, cluttered patio, frightened. A scorpion had stung a goat the day before, and I had given her a shot of antitoxin. She was a mother. I was afraid that something had gone wrong and that her little kids were orphans.

Don Paco said it again as I got near enough to see the goat clearly. It was hanging by its left hind foot from a limb of the Jerusalem thorn, the hens' nesting tree.

"Look. A goat died this morning."

Then he lifted the goat's left front leg.

"From a knife," he said. "Right here."

I woke up and remembered what day it was. It was the birthday of Chela's two nieces, both named Luz: Luz Campos and Luz Forsythe. Today they were both fifteen.

I had been vaguely aware in Guadalajara that a fifteenth birth-day was special. One could hardly overlook the notices on the society pages of the newspapers or the frothy dresses in the shops specializing in apparel for brides and fifteen-year-olds. But it took Jesús María to give me an idea of what a fifteenth birthday could mean to a girl, especially if her aunt were Chela.

I was curious, at first, to know why both girls were named Luz.

"Were they named for the same grandmother or something?" I asked Chela.

She gave me the puzzled look she so often gave me when I betrayed my ignorance.

"They're both named Luz because they both had the luck to be born on the twenty-second of May," she told me.

"So?"

"It's one of the special days of the Virgin," she said kindly. "Their whole name is Maria de la Luz." Mary of the Light.

"Oh," I said. "What a beautiful name."

I thought a minute.

"And a girl can't be named Maria de la Luz if she doesn't have the luck to be born on the twenty-second of May?"

"We're always named for the saint whose day we're born on," Chela said gently, pitying me.

"Oh," I said. "Boys, too?"

"Of course."

I thought some more. "And if a girl is born on the day of a man saint, or a boy...."

Then I remembered the names that had charmed me. There were girls named Tomasa and Alfreda, and, yes, there were boys named Margarito and Virginio. Sometimes the parents didn't bother to change the sex of the names. There was a Beatriz in Jesús María and, yes, an Isabel, both young men.

For the two girls named Luz, there would be a special Mass today, a party dinner, and a real dance afterward. Don Paco was so pleased at the prospect of a fiesta that he could kill a goat and make jokes about it before the sun came up.

Luz Campos was the daughter of Chela's sister Inez, and a charming girl, but I was really more interested in Luz Forsythe, Arcelia's daughter, the tall one. Her uncle, her father's brother, had brought her down to Tepic from Chihuahua, where he had had her in school, and Chela had dragooned me into bringing her out on the plane from Tepic.

"She's almost fourteen now," Chela told me at the time. "Old enough so some man could rob her."

I knew enough of the vernacular to know that "rob" meant a four-letter word my mother would have pronounced "violate."

"On the plane?" I protested.

"You don't know Mexicans," Chela had replied darkly.

So I had driven through the back streets of Tepic to find the house where Luz's grandfather lived, her Mexican grandfather with the Scottish surname, and there had arranged to meet Luz the next morning at the airport. Her uncle from Chihuahua delivered her. He questioned me closely to make sure, I thought, that I was competent to deliver her safely home.

She was a pretty girl, with her shiny brown hair and greenish-brown eyes. Chela pointed out to me later that her skin was very fair, but this I did not remark at the time. I was not as conscious of the color of people's skin as Mexicans seemed to be except to notice that, in contrast to the mountain people, my friends from the States kept looking more and more peaked.

Arcelia's husband, Luz's father, was dead. He had been a sewing-machine repairman when Arcelia married him, working in Tepic. There they had lived in a pretty, modern house with running water and a washing machine. There Arcelia didn't have to go down to the river to wash clothes in the burning sun.

"There I was white. White," she told me.

But eventually her father, Perez, had asked Arcelia and her husband to bring their three children out to Jesús María to live. El Señor Perez had no sons and needed a son-in-law to help him. Inez's husband had left her. Juana's husband, Gustavo, had cattle and other affairs of his own. Chela was not yet married. So Arcelia and her husband obligingly exchanged their comfortable city life for the rigors of life in the mountains.

Arcelia's husband knew nothing of the Sierra, but he quickly learned. Soon Arcelia's father was sending him out on really important errands. The last one was to buy fifty head of cattle on certain ranchos far to the north in the mountains. Arcelia's husband left with a bagful of pesos and never came back.

It wasn't long before three Indians turned up in Tepic and began spending money wildly and getting very drunk. They were picked up by the police. It would be better not to ask what means were used to get a confession out of them, but, as a result of the confession, Arcelia's husband's body was found at the bottom of the ravine where the three Indians had thrown him after they had robbed and murdered him.

"I was queer for a long time after that," Arcelia told me. "I couldn't remember anything."

Arcelia now had a poor, crumbly little house across The Street of San Miguel from Chela's with a few things in it to sell, bought on Chela's credit. With some help from Chela, she managed to feed two hungry boys and Luz, but she had no money to send Luz on to secondary school. It was a federal school and cost a pittance, but Arcelia couldn't afford it. With an ardent conviction that education is *all*, I had insisted that Luz enter and had offered to pay the tiny tuition. With her usual grace, Arcelia accepted, and Luz continued her education with resident Coras, visiting Huichols, and a few hometown mestizos.

Today Luz was fifteen, and for several weeks it had been obvious that a very eligible young man was in love with her. He was the youthful veterinary who had arrived to coordinate the services now offered by the government, chiefly in agronomy and veterinary science. His offices were in the federal building downriver, the building through which the water had poured during the flood.

He was a stocky young man, Jaime by name, with a round cheerful face and big horn–rimmed glasses, and he couldn't keep his eyes off Luz. He was an inch shorter than Luz, but so were most of the other youths in Jesús María. He was also a proper young man. In place of enticing Luz down to the river, he was manfully trying to persuade Arcelia to permit him to court her. We teased about it, but Arcelia scoffed delicately.

"How ridiculous," she said. "Luz isn't fifteen yet, and the doctor is a city boy." Arcelia always called him "the doctor." Chela did, too. "His family has a fine house in Guadalajara. What would they want with a little *ranchera*, or she with them!"

I believed that Arcelia was thinking, too, that she would not be losing a daughter to a neighbor boy there in Jesús María but to a young man from away who would surely leave Jesús María eventually, taking Luz with him. Arcelia had already lost enough.

Still, Arcelia was charming to Jaime when he came to sit and chat with her in the dark little room with the unplastered adobe walls, the makeshift counter of planks laid on sawhorses spread with costume jewelry, batteries, embroidery floss, and printed kerchiefs. The room was so small there was scarcely space in it for two rickety chairs and a barrel, and it smelled leathery from the huaraches hanging at eye level from a rafter at the side of the room.

Arcelia always sat in one of the chairs, rising to make an occasional sale of warm Pepsi. Jaime would perch on the barrel. If Luz came in, she would glance at the doctor aslant out of her greenish-brown eyes and slide quickly out of the room.

"He's so old," she told Chela. "He's almost twenty-two."

But today was no day to think about Jaime and his apparently hopeless suit. Today was the day when Luz Campos and Luz Forsythe were both fifteen. Today they were going to have a fiesta they would remember for the rest of their lives. Preparations for it had been, to say the least, impressive.

They had started two weeks before when Chela's sala, her living room, was suddenly littered with yellow and white tissue paper, yellow and white stiff paper, yellow and white crepe paper, and wire.

Aside from my room with the window on the street, Chela's sala was the only room in Chela's whole compound that boasted a window. The room opened onto the patio with a small, skull-cracking door and also into the store, which occasionally overflowed. The window opened onto the street and attracted voyeurs.

The sala was a small room but stuffed with furniture: a varnished chiffonnier with carving glued on, a gilt and imitation marble table covered with knickknacks, a sofa and two upholstered chairs covered with transparent plastic, a small shrine. The walls were covered with framed pictures of various saints, the Holy Family, and Chela herself as a bride looking soulful.

Seven girls crowded into the sweltering little room, finding
places to sit on the floor to make paper flowers. The work was inter-
rupted just long enough for a conference about clothes.

The gowns of Luz Campos and Luz Forsythe had been hanging
under sheets in their respective houses for a month, but the *damas*
were still to be accoutred. The damas were the attendants who were
to precede the fifteen-year-olds down the aisle in the church. Most
girls were satisfied with one or two damas, Chela told me, but she insisted that her nieces have one dama for every saint's day they had
celebrated since their birth. She picked the damas herself: one one-
year-old dama, one two-year-old dama, one three-year-old dama,
and so on up to the elderly dama of fourteen.

Chela piled up the paper-flower makings in the corner of the sala
long enough for the clothes conference with the older damas and the
mothers of the younger ones. She had drawn fourteen sketches of a
dress with a tight bodice and a full, ankle-length skirt. She distributed the sketches. Then she got out a bolt of sky-blue dotted swiss
she had bought in Tepic and cut off appropriate lengths for each
dama. Businesswoman as always, she charged for the material, but
only a little more than she had paid. The mothers went home with
their fabric and sketches, and the girls pulled the paper and wire out
of the corner and got back to work.

As the birthday grew near, the preparations accelerated. The
older damas, sweating copiously, strung long garlands of paper
flowers, yellow and white, on strong cord threaded through drinking
straws to keep the flowers apart. Padre Domingo helped Chela and
Luz Campos festoon the church with flowery lassoes from the high
hanging chandelier to the spikes in the walls.

Luz Forsythe arranged the white paper roses with the long wire
stems in the aged gray urns in front of the new altar, and yellow and
white daisies in the shiny new fruit-juice cans on the old one. Jaime
hopefully offered his help, and Luz politely declined it.

Don Paco rode off on his handsome mule and returned with a
goat from the rancho. It bleated pitifully in the corral behind the
house, where it stayed three days to purify itself.

On the dawn of the great day, Don Paco hung the goat on the
Jerusalem thorn tree and began delicately to skin it. Chela's dogs circled him nervously, sniffing.

Little Panchillo of the lop-eared burro joyfully roped the resident hens and jailed them in the abandoned henhouse in the corral behind the compound.

As the sun came up, Chela emerged from the bedroom with a lavender chiffon scarf around her curlers and began sweeping the packed earth of the long, untidy patio.

Chela's sisters arrived to help.

Juana slipped into the kitchen and began grinding corn in the handmill. The gate squeaked to announce the arrival of one of the damas, who washed her hands in the kitchen trough and began kneading the tortilla dough.

Arcelia floated into the kitchen and began preparing the *birria* sauce with four kinds of chile, chocolate, cloves, oregano, bay leaf, and goodness knows what else.

A girl I had never seen before stood behind the flat mud stove, flipping tortillas from the hot clay griddle into a huge basket lined with an elaborately embroidered cloth.

Two Franciscan nuns visiting in Jesús María had baked a cake in the curato's outdoor oven. It towered on the kitchen table, layer on lopsided layer, iced with jam and decorated with pink flowers.

Jaime quietly entered through the store and the sala and asked what he could do to help. Arcelia sent him to bring more wood.

Don Paco was in charge of the birria. First, he cut up the goat with a great wicked knife. Then he built a carefully laid fire in the middle of three large stones at the far end of the patio. He brought a cauldron from the storeroom and put the cut-up goat in it, along with the sauce Arcelia had made. Then he sealed down the lid around the edges with tortilla dough and put a heavy stone on top of the lid.

Jaime loitered in the patio, solid, cheerful, and undismayed.

All the chairs and tables in Chela's compound found their way into the patio. Chela breezed into my house with Felipe and Julian, Arcelia's big teenage sons.

"Excuse me," she said breezily, as she appropriated my two tables and three chairs. Jaime helped line them all up and down the middle of the patio.

The two fifteen-year-olds and three damas were fidgeting in the sala. Chela went in and set their hair. The sala smelled strongly of permanent-wave lotion.

The Mass was not to be until five, but the musicians arrived at noon: two guitarists, a violinist, and a short, fat man with a bass guitar. They started playing at once, Mexican country music with its curlicues on the violin and plucking on the bass. They put down their instruments long enough for beans and tortillas and then played on again.

As soon as Chela stopped being beautician, she started to be bustling housewife again. She pulled lavishly embroidered tablecloths out of the chiffonnier and spread them on the tables. She laid places with the big, flat bowls that served as dinner plates in Jesús María and with the tablespoons with which we ate everything. She worried about the glassware. Should she put out the twelve crystal goblets, she wondered, for the special guests at the end of the table? She did.

She carefully laid a paper napkin beside each bowl. I had tried to buy some in her store when I first moved in, but she had told me, "We haven't any to sell. People don't use napkins here." She laughed. "Except for wedding dinners."

Felipe, Julian, and Jaime made benches along the sides of the table where the supply of chairs gave out. They laid planks between supports made of wooden crates. Everything was ready for the feast.

At 3:30, guests arrived from Arroyo Santiago. There were eight of them, five women and three men. The women had blankets over their saddles, which they wrapped around their legs from back to front for modesty. The men held the bridles of the women's mules while the women dismounted and adjusted their skirts.

Don Paco at once took the gentlemen to my end of the patio and began opening beer cans. They were floating in a washtub of water, but such was the heat of the day that the beer had to be warm.

Chela pulled chairs into the shade of the mesquite tree for the women and then hurried into the living room to comb hair. The damas were waiting and watched as she undid Luz Campos's rollers and pulled her hair down into long corkscrew curls. One by one, she combed the hair of all the others, ending with Luz Forsythe, pulling out curlers, teasing hair, and rolling it into elaborate puffs and whorls. As each girl's hair was tortured into a creation, the girl herself slipped out of the sala and hustled home to dress. The sala smelled strongly of lacquer and hair spray. It was now almost five o'clock.

Impossible as it had seemed beforehand, everybody got ready early enough so the Mass could be on time (Mexican time, that is: only fifteen minutes late). The damas, from little one-year-old Marina to fourteen-year-old Lucia, all congregated back in Chela's patio in their sky-blue dresses with the long, full skirts. On their heads they had chaplets of blue plastic flowers Chela had bought in Tepic. On their feet they had new white shoes their mothers had bought from Chela.

Luz Campos arrived in a long pink dress from her older brother who lived in Colorado, the nephew for whom Chela had built my house. Luz Forsythe was in butter yellow. Chela had bought her dress in an expensive shop in Puerto Vallarta. Both girls wore lacy white picture hats and new white gloves.

Chela lined the girls up, the tiniest in front, the two Marias de la Luz at the back, and they all filed down to the church, with Chela bending down to hold the hand of Marina, the one-year-old. Chela had attired herself in splendor, too. Her hair, out of its curlers, hung in ringlets under her black lace mananita. She was wearing a fashion-able hot silk dress from Guadalajara, soft green and becoming.

The guests, the musicians, Don Paco, Jaime, and I watched in ad-miration as the girls, little to big, in single file, stepped carefully along in their new white shoes, looking dainty and sweet in their sky-blue dresses against the rough brown adobe of the houses, the rough brown stones of the road. Even the spotted pig at the side of the road stopped rooting and snorting to gaze at them.

The Mass was a pretty ceremony. The church looked very festive with its homemade decorations. The girls looked solemn and charm-ing, and Padre Domingo was at his most engaging. Chela had ex-plained the significance of the Mass beforehand.

"It's a Mass of thanksgiving," she told me. "A girl gives thanks to God that she has stayed alive for fifteen years, that she hasn't died. For a girl, her fifteenth-year Mass is almost as glorious as a wedding."

The church was full and suffocating, but only Don Paco seemed to be suffering. The empty beer cans around the washtub testified to the warmth of his hospitality. He sat, and stood, and knelt through the Mass, mopping his face and looking desperate. The rest of us fanned ourselves, but nobody fainted.

Jaime gazed at Arcelia's Luz from the beginning to the end of the Mass. I wondered if he were seeing her through his big horn-rimmed glasses not in her expensive yellow dress from Puerto Vallarta but in a chaste white wedding gown.

After the Mass and the picture-taking in front of the church, we thronged back to Chela's patio. As Chela said later, half the town was there, and the other half was insulted not to have been invited. She was referring to the part of town up the river. There was just one Cora at the fiesta, just Arnulfo Flores. Not only was he Presidente Municipal, but his son, the teacher, was one of Chela's countless godsons.

The musicians were playing lustily as we streamed through the gate into Chela's patio, still Mexican country music with its falsetto cackles and instrumental furbelows. The sun was just setting behind the mountain.

Chela seated us at the long table, Luz Campos and Luz Forsythe together at the head. I was lucky enough to draw a chair. The little visiting nun who sat next to me admired the tablecloth.

"Whoever embroidered this was a lot of woman," she said.

The birria was delicious, the tortillas were moist and hot, the music was loud, there was plenty of brandy to put in the Pepsi Cola, and the two Luzes ate the whole dinner and cut the cake with their white gloves still on. Guests who were not given seats were given plates and ate where they stood. Two of Chela's goblets got broken. It was a very merry gathering.

It kept on being merry all night. Chela's sisters carried the dishes to the kitchen, and Padre Domingo helped move the tables and chairs to around the edges of the patio. Then, discreetly and, I thought, reluctantly, he went back to the curato. Chela offered me a chair, but I, in a self-sacrificing mood, sat down on a bench at the side of the earthen dance floor.

The sky darkened and the moon came up. More guests arrived. It looked as if every young man from Jesús María and the ranchos round about had clustered under the Jerusalem thorn tree, their hats blobs of white in the shadow. Jaime took his place among them. Mules and horses slept on their feet outside the gate, occasionally stamping.

More girls slipped in through the gate to sit beside me on the bench, all in their modest Sunday dresses except for the two young schoolteachers from Tepic. They were both spectacular in hip huggers and tank tops, one of which read in English, "Blood Sweat and Tears," and the other, "Love Love Love."

When the bench was full, the dancing began. As at the wedding up at El Cerro, a young man strode from the group under the tree, grabbed a girl by the wrist, yanked her to her feet, and started dancing. Another followed him, and another. They danced without talking, each looking seriously into the distance, the young men still wearing their big white hats, some with knives on their rumps.

Luz Campos and Luz Forsythe both took their hats off for the dancing. For two young people dancing together, one hat was enough. Mostly they sat in chairs looking queenly. Their elegant dresses were too long to dance in, and their new white shoes too tight.

After a decent interval, Jaime came out from under the tree, bowed formally to Luz Forsythe, and apparently asked for a dance. She turned her head away, declining.

Don Gustavo came and snatched me to my feet to dance a wild, whirling caper. Everybody laughed. Having seen the same setup at the wedding, I should have known that the bench was meant only for señoritas. My sitting on it had embarrassed everybody until Don Gustavo came to my rescue.

At what seemed to me a reasonable hour—in other words, midnight—I slipped off to my bed, virtually the only piece of furniture left in my little house. Every time I woke up, which I did rather frequently owing to the hullabaloo in the patio, the musicians were playing louder and the laughter was merrier. Finally, as it began to get light, I stopped trying to sleep. The musicians were still playing, but the guests from Arroyo Santiago were loudly trying to revive Don Paco to bid him good–bye.

I thought I knew what would happen on this new day. Chela, I thought, would probably spend the day in bed, occasionally moaning. Luz Campos and Luz Forsythe and some of the damas, all in modish dresses from Tepic and Guadalajara, would swagger out of the gate with plastic washtubs on their heads full of dirty dishes to wash in the river. Don Paco would sit behind the counter in the cluttered little store with a brutal headache. Jaime would slip into the house across the street to talk to Arcelia and look at Luz when she came back from the river. I would have to carry my chairs and tables home myself.

Still, it had been a wonderful celebration–indeed, almost as glorious as a wedding. I wouldn't have missed it for the world. I was, to be sure, guiltily glad that it would be three years before another of Chela's nieces turned fifteen. I was sorry, though, that none of the others could be named Maria de la Luz. None of the others had had the luck to be born on the twenty-second of May.

16

The Tail of the Noble Mule

On July 25 came the feast of Saint James, Santo Santiago, the apostle who was fervently believed to have appeared on his white horse to rally the Spanish to victory in decisive battles against the Moors. He was appropriately revered, and a spirited fiesta celebrated his saint's day, in Jesús María.

I had seen it the previous year and did not care to see it again. It featured horsemen, two racing abreast, and roosters decorated with paper roses in blue, pink, and yellow. One horseman held the rooster by the feet; the other grasped its head. With their horses pounding up The Street in Front of the Church, the two riders twirled the bird between them until its head came off.

Meantime, one or more Coras danced on the *tarima,* a drumlike platform set up under a mesquite tree. The noise was deafening close by and audible all the way up and down the town.

In Arroyo Santiago, there was going to be a gentler kind of fiesta, a fiesta to install a statue of Santo Santiago, the settlement's patron saint.

Arroyo Santiago was three hours away from Jesús María, over some of the most beautiful mountains anywhere. I had gone to it once before, earlier in the summer. It was a pretty little settlement on the leafy bank of a small river that never ran dry. It had a tiny church, a one-room school, and several houses of rock and adobe placed here and there among the trees. Oddly enough, there in the middle of the Cora zone, most of the inhabitants were Huichols. One of them, Don José Manuel, often came to see me in Jesús María, always in his spotless white muslins gorgeously embroidered with eagles, deer, and butterflies. He was an older man, a courtly man, José Manuel, and always kissed my hand when he saluted me. I asked him once how it happened that there was a whole colony of Huichols there in Cora country.

"It was the revolution," he told me. "Everybody went up to the mountaintops. When the war was over, my father and some of the others forgot which way they had come from and came down on the wrong side of the mountain. It was nice here by the water so they stayed."

I wasn't sure I believed him, but it was a good story.

There was one Cora family there, too. It was a prosperous family, with a good house in Jesús María as well. There were also some mestizos, a merry group with handsome young men in it who had been instrumental in amassing the money to give to the bishop so he could buy them a statue of Santo Santiago. They had organized dances in Jesús María and Santa Rosa, a rodeo in La Guerra, a bull-throwing contest somewhere else, I was told, and fairs everywhere. Every event had its queen, the best money-maker of all.

The youths would pick out two girls, two nominees. Two boxes would appear on the counters of all the stores. Each box would have a name of one of the girls on it and a slot into which everyone was urged to insert legal tender. The girl who amassed the most money got the queen's cape, the queen's crown, and the queen's chair at whatever the event might be. All the money went toward the purchase of the statue of Santo Santiago.

The statue itself rested for three weeks in the curato, in a dark corner of a storeroom with sheets, towels, sacks of beans, and rolls of toilet paper. Padre Jacinto had flown it out right to the now almost abandoned airstrip on the flats by the river, and Fray Nicolas and a Cora named Gaspar had carried it up the hill.

The statue was, to tell the truth, a little disappointing. It was smaller than life-size, and, although the figures of Saint James and his banner were pretty good, Saint James's horse looked as if it had been modeled by somebody who had heard a horse described but had never seen one. It looked pitifully undernourished and had a long, thin, arched neck supporting a big head with a Roman nose. It rested on a litter with carrying shafts at each end.

We started out on July 23 in the early afternoon, two Huichols carrying the litter with Saint James on it, the statue itself teetering a little as the men stepped over the rocks and into the gullies. Two Cora boys followed on foot with rockets, then I on a borrowed mule. We had a small contingent of perhaps six or seven other Coras and Huichols, both on foot and on mules, and one young mestizo on a very fractious horse. Every few minutes, one of the Cora boys would light a rocket in his bare hand. It would hiss for a moment and then boom in the sky. I would jump almost out of my saddle, but the mule, hardened by long experience, would plod on imperturbably.

I had gone over the same trail once before. It was just after the rains started. The mestizos in Arroyo Santiago were relations of Chela and took care of her and Don Paco's cattle farther up in the mountains. One of them had come to Chela's store to ask me to go home with him, as his wife was sick. I would have to spend the night.

He was one of the handsomest youths of Arroyo Santiago, this young husband. Chela introduced him as Antonio, and he smiled engagingly as he gave me his wife's symptoms. She obviously had a urinary infection, for some reason common among mestizas in the Sierra. (I thought privately it was because they slept with all their clothes on, including their underpants.)

Antonio accompanied me to Padre Domingo's clinic, and I stuffed the medicines I thought his wife would need into one of my woven Cora bags. Then the two of us went together to the Health Center. We were between doctors, and Padre Domingo was away, but I had Antonio recite his wife's symptoms to Don Serafim, who approved my selections, scolded Antonio, and hoped that God would go with us.

I stopped at the store to ask Chela from whom I should borrow a mule, as Antonio had not brought me one. Chela at once offered me her own *macho*, her male mule. He was famous for his good manners.

I put on my slacks, common sense winning over concern for public approval, while Don Paco saddled the mule.

"You'll need a nylon," Chela said anxiously. A nylon was a big plastic sheet. "Look at those clouds. It's going to rain."

The clouds were, indeed, rolling up from the north, purple and menacing.

"I'll take my umbrella," I said smugly and went back to get it.

Chela and Don Paco looked on, unbelievingly, as Antonio and I started off–I with a small, folding umbrella dangling from the pommel of my saddle. My follies sometimes left them speechless.

The rain didn't slam down on us for nearly an hour. Before it did, Antonio unrolled a big sheet of plastic he had tied on behind his saddle and covered himself with it completely: hat, shoulders, hands, saddle, huaraches. I slipped my umbrella from the pommel and managed to open it before the first big drops hurled themselves upon me. My umbrella was inside out, and I was drenched from head to foot, in seconds.

We plodded on. The trail was more traveled than some in the mountains and thus less hazardous, but the downpour turned it into rock–bottomed little rivers on the slopes and to slush in the hollows. The rain was like an assault, and the macho and I both pushed into it with our heads bent over.

Eventually, the rain stopped. I was too miserable in my sopping clothes to appreciate the beauty of the mountains through and over which we were riding. They were green, lush, and beflowered. Another day, I told myself, another day.

At last we reached the trail down the side of the mountain, across the river from Arroyo Santiago. The footing was of deep, slippery mud. The trail itself got narrower and narrower. Chela's macho eyed it suspiciously, head down, as he took one tentative step after another. Finally, Antonio dismounted, giving his mule a slap.

"Here we walk a little," he said, smiling back at me.

I clumsily climbed down from the macho. Luckily, the drop down to the river was on the right side of the trail, so, in dismounting, I was next to the mountain wall, which rose up on the left side of the animal. As Antonio led the macho on ahead, I crept down the trail behind him, clutching the sparse grass that grew on the side of the mountain. When we reached the little river, I mounted again to cross over to Antonio's house and his sick wife.

Her condition was far from grave, and I knew that, with the medicine, she would soon be flipping tortillas again. I, hungry and miserable in my wet clothes, went early to bed in the kareton. Rolled up in the cotton blanket Antonio had lent me, I lay shivering on the kareton's corrugated bamboo floor, waiting for the cocks to crow the hours: eleven o'clock, then one o'clock, then three o'clock. At five o'clock, stiff from the saddle and with my clothes still wet, I climbed down the notched log and lumbered over to Antonio's cook house.

A little boy was found to accompany me back to Jesús María. My *pistolero*, they said. At the bad place in the trail, he dismounted and told me to do the same. I did. But this time, the river was down below on the left side of the macho. I flung my right leg over his back and stepped on the edge of the trail. It was black mush. My right foot sank farther and farther down the side of the mountain; my left knee, with my left foot still in the stirrup, rose nearer and nearer my nose. There was no way I could pull myself up by the saddle, which I was clutching frantically. I let go of the cantle long enough to grab the macho by the tail. He was so well brought up he didn't even flinch. I managed to get his tail in both my hands, to get my foot out of the stirrup, and to pull myself up behind my saintly mount and, from there, up to the right side of the narrow trail.

"A woman slid down there and got killed a couple of years ago," my pistolero told me amiably as he led my macho up to safe ground.

From then on, the ride back to Jesús María in my sticky clothes was miserable but uneventful. Chela said when I got home, "No nylon! And you didn't even take a blanket or a change of clothes!"

Some people learn the hard way.

Making the trip with Santo Santiago and his escort was a great deal more dignified, except for the rockets. I had a nylon, my sleeping bag, two changes of clothes, my flashlight, soap, towel, and toothbrush, all but the sleeping bag in my rucksack. I also had two cartons of medicine, which obliging Huichols tied on the backs of their saddles.

When we arrived in Arroyo Santiago, the statue was respectfully put under the wild fig tree beside the church, and the Huichols asked me where I would like them to put the medicine. Nobody offered me a bed, so I told the young men to put the boxes in the schoolhouse. The school had one room, a dirt floor, a small blackboard, one bench, and two tables, both of them dirty, as it was vacation time.

I cleaned off the tables, unpacked, and spread out the medicine on one of them and my sleeping bag on the other. Then the inhabitants began to swarm in with their greetings, embraces, sores, worms, amoebas, scabies, and ugly burns from exploding rockets. I was busy until after dark.

A city block down the path from the school, there was the house of a mestizo with a Huichol wife. He had invited me to supper. The batteries of my flashlight went dead. I had not yet learned to take extra batteries with me, and I knew there wasn't a battery for sale in all of Arroyo Santiago, but I was hungry. Stumbling in the dark, I reached the path that led to the mestizo's house. I waited until someone came along who did have a flashlight. After the beans and tortillas in the lean-to kitchen of the mestizo, two laughing Huichol girls grabbed me and ran me at top speed back through the dark night, right to the school.

Five men had built a fire in front of the door. I couldn't see who they were. They were cooking the cow they had killed that afternoon, the Huichol girls told me. We said good-night all the way around, and I groped my way to the table with my sleeping bag on it. It was a Mexican sleeping bag with a covering of dressy peach-colored nylon, very slippery. After I got into it, I reflected that, aside from the imminent danger of slipping off the table, I had never felt safer in my life.

The bishop rode in the next day, accompanied by a visiting nun from Tepic and a couple of Coras. I was so busy with the sick and hurt in the schoolhouse that I didn't even know who put them up, or where. There was a ceremony under the wild fig in the afternoon, which I attended. The bishop blessed the statue of Santo Santiago and invited the faithful to confession.

Mass was the next morning, the feast day of the patron saint. The church was full. Huichols had arrived from the surrounding hills. The Cora family was there with other visiting Coras and with Chela's mestizo relations. The music, as usual, was dismal and the singing very thin, as only the mestizos knew the tunes and the words. The bishop, big, kind, and majestic, preached a simple sermon, again so slowly that even I could understand every word.

Only one person took Communion: the visiting nun from Tepic. Only she had confessed.

The bishop was not pleased. Nobody expected the Indians to confess or take Communion. They availed themselves of baptism for their children and the bishop's generosity for themselves, but they had their own compact with God. Arroyo Santiago, however, had mestizos, and the bishop well knew that they had plenty of sins to atone for. He himself was as close to the mortal sin of anger as I ever saw him. He announced that he would be available for confessions after the service and that there would be another Mass in the afternoon to permit those who had abstained to take Communion.

I went back to my dwindling supply of medicine and my growing number of patients. The handsome young mestizos—those who had organized all the functions to buy the statue—leapt on their mules and lightheartedly rode away. I was told that in Santa Rosa there was a man who sold tequila.

Don José Manuel, elegant and courtly as ever, was among the Huichols who slept in the schoolhouse that night. When I got back from supper with the mestizo and his wife, there were sixteen of them, men, women, children, and babies, rolled up in their blankets on the soft dirt floor José Manuel's flashlight had batteries. He held it on my sleeping bag so I could slide into it and zip it up. Then he moved the bench to a spot in front of my table, between me and the sleeping Huichols. There he slept all night rolled up in his own blanket, my knight and my protector. As if I needed one.

The next day, we rode back to Jesús María, the bishop, the nun, the two Coras, and I. The rains had held off for several days, and the trails were firm and dry, even along the side of the mountain where Chela's macho had saved me from sliding down to the rocks and the river. The Sierra was beautiful, unimaginably green, with the flowers of August bursting out of the buds of July, yellow and orange in the hollows, red and violet near the peaks.

It was late afternoon when we rode down The Street in Front of the Church in Jesús María. There were fourteen ponies munching the leaves from last year's cornstalks as we passed by a corral. The road was littered a little, here and there, with tattered paper roses in pink, blue, and yellow—and with chicken feathers. Somebody was dancing on the tarima, thundering out a rhythm on the square wooden drum.

There were two buckets of water waiting for me in my house. After a dish of beans and a cup of coffee with Chela, I bathed out of one bucket and dumped my three-day-old clothes in the other. My clean clothes were still in the rucksack. In Arroyo Santiago, there had been no place to change.

I stretched out gratefully on my native bed. After three nights in a slippery sleeping bag on a wooden table, my bamboo mat suspended between two sawhorses felt like an innerspring mattress or, better still, a feather bed.

17

The Hospital Harbors an Indian Village

The first time I saw Piedad, she was lying face down on the table in the lofty, crumbling room where we kept the medicine. She was stark naked and was burned from her hair, frizzed by the fire, almost to the soles of her small, neat, dirty feet. She was a Cora, nine or ten years old, I figured, a tall little girl, and strong.

Padre Domingo was away, and I had come to see if I could help the nurse we had acquired. She had been in Jesús María five days, a fine, hearty nun who had been working for several years in equatorial Africa. I was greatly enjoying the respite she was giving me, but I did drop in every morning to see if there was anything I could do to help her.

On this morning, she was carefully lifting off tissue-thin strips of loose skin from Piedad's burned back with a small pair of forceps. Piedad was not uttering a sound.

Chuy and six or seven other Coras were standing around watching the nun, horrified. Piedad's mother was sitting on the floor, leaning against the leg of the table with her baby, wrapped in her black rebozo, asleep in her arms. She was explaining.

"We were bringing the pig to town to sell it. I had matches, and Piedad said couldn't we make a fire and warm up a little." (December mornings can be cold, and it was now December.) "There was wood there on the flats by the river, so we made a fire. Piedad was warming her back, and her dress began to burn. It burned right up the back. Gaspar was there, and he threw his blanket around her. The flames went up and down. I tore her clothes off her, and we ran up here."

By some inexplicable miracle, Padre Jacinto had flown into Jesús María that morning, two days ahead of time. His little Cessna was right down on the flats. Nobody else landed a plane there anymore because the abutment of the footbridge protruded into what had been the airstrip. The padre, however, kept on landing his plane there as he had done before. It was said that he would land almost any-where if someone needed help. The moment I saw Piedad, I realized that there could be nobody anywhere who needed help more than she did. How the padre could have known was a matter I never in-quired into.

I had met him going out of the burros' door as I was going in. He had said we ought to take that little girl to Tepic and had stridden off on some errand of his own.

When I saw Piedad, I was as horrified as the Coras. I had never seen such a burn in all my life. Finally, I found my voice.

"Please get me a clean sheet," I said to the nun. "We must take this child to Tepic."

The worthy nun, too good tempered to be affronted by my de-mand, put down her forceps and ran for a sheet. The padre came back just in time to help me lift the little girl onto it. Then he carried her down to the flats. I climbed into the plane; the padre put the child in my lap, face down, and climbed into the pilot's seat.

Piedad's mother had followed us. She stood beside the plane clutching her baby in her arms and crying as Padre Jacinto started the motor and we teetered down the gravel, picked up speed, and took off to skim up the canyon and over the mountaintops.

The little girl squirmed. Before I knew how she had contrived to do it, she was sitting up in my lap, her whole hideously burned back resting against the sheet that was enfolding her. How she could bear the pain, sitting that way, I could not imagine. It was some time before I was told that there is very little sensation in a third-degree burn.

She leaned far over to look through the window, peering down. Then, "My house," she said. "There it is. My house."

I peered down, too, and saw it. There were two tiny thatched roofs in the thicket of shrubs and underbrush. There was a small cor-ral beside it and below it the river, narrow and blue.

"And you can see my goat," Piedad said. "My baby goat. The goat my father gave me."

She was crying.

She smelled. She smelled of charred flesh and burned hair.

She smelled of little Cora girl who hadn't been bathed that morning. And she was crying.

In Tepic, the padre drove us from the airport to the hospital in the Franciscan pickup truck. He carried Piedad inside, with me following meekly after. Not stopping to speak to anyone, he strode down the hall, nudged open a door to what proved to be the women's ward, carefully laid Piedad face down on an empty bed, and left, saying as he did so that he would speak to the mother superior. I was alone with a child so badly burned I was not sure she could live through the night.

I had supposed that I would leave the child in the care of the hospital doctors and nurses and that I would head for the Franciscan hostel, checking in at the hospital every day during visiting hours. It took about five minutes to discover that, in a Mexican hospital, one does not deposit a patient and walk away.

There in the women's ward were fourteen beds. Only eight of them were occupied, but each occupant had at least one relation and sometimes more than one there to take care of her. The relatives bathed their sick, took charge of the bedpan, fed the patient if she was too weak to feed herself, adjusted her pillow, helped the nurse change her sheets, and slept on the tile floor beside her bed.

I was obviously to be Piedad's "relation," and I didn't even know who she was.

I soon learned. I was bending over her when a soft voice asked me, "What is the little girl's name?"

I looked up to see one of the kindest faces I had ever seen, thin, lined, and pale but with large, luminous eyes that deserved the debased adjective "compassionate." It was the mother superior. The padre had indeed spoken to her. In her nurse's uniform and her nun's white veil, she looked to me very much like an angel.

"I am Piedad Garcia Mejia, and I want to go home," Piedad said clearly, screwing her head around to glare at the mother superior.

"And I am Madre Dolores," the mother superior said gently. "We hope you will like it here."

A lay nurse came with the madre; Fernanda, she said her name was. She flinched when she saw how the burn extended into Piedad's armpits and even her crotch. She brought me a clean blanket to cover Piedad and then went to her station at the end of the room to prepare shots. I had a feeling that she had even less hope for Piedad than I had.

The room had a hospital smell of antiseptics, of piney soap with which the floor was scrubbed, of alcohol. It was a bright, turquoise-blue room with one whole side in windows that looked out on roses blooming pinkly over a garden wall. Piedad had squirmed onto her back. She looked around her at the big, bright room full of white beds, at the strange light-colored people all so different from her soft, dark mother, at the woman bending over her. White.

I took one of her hands in my own. She snatched it away.

Fernanda, down at her station, had washed her hands with soap and now was cleaning under her nails with gauze soaked in alcohol. The nurses, I was discovering, did everything that required professional training. They gave the shots, the I.V.'s, the bandaging after surgery, everything that needed special knowledge and an expert hand—and never in any hospital had I ever seen hands so clean. All the other nurses, like Fernanda, prepared to give shots as if they were on their way to the operating table.

The room had gone quiet when Padre Jacinto strode in. Nobody had spoken since, not to me, not to Madre Dolores, nor to each other. But as soon as Fernanda started on her rounds with the wheeled tray of hypodermic syringes, the chatter began.

"Ah, Fernanda, no shot this afternoon."

"Roll over fast, or I'll give you two." Everybody laughed.

"Fernanda," in a matter-of-fact voice, "it hurts where the doctor operated."

"I know, my queen. We'll turn you over gently, gently. The shot will stop the pain."

"Fernanda, give the shot to my sister. She needs it more than I do."

The sister, burlesquing, clutched her rump and sidled away. Everybody laughed again.

After she had given all the shots, Fernanda came back to look at

Piedad. Piedad looked back. Her eyes were dark and hostile, her mouth turned down in scorn.

"Who is she?" Fernanda asked.

"A little Cora girl," I said.

"Where is her mother?"

"Back in the mountains," I said.

"And her father?"

"I don't know."

"My father is at the coast," Piedad said, very distinctly. "He is working there."

"They're terribly poor," I told Fernanda.

Fernanda looked sympathetic and went to check two I.V.'s.

Piedad raised her head.

"*No somos pobres,*" she hissed at me. "We are not poor. We have shrimp from the river to fill that bowl," pointing to the jug on a neighboring bed table. "My father grows tomatoes, and cabbages, and beans. He has a cornfield up on the mountain, and we have corn. Lots of corn. And I have a goat. A baby goat. My father gave it to me."

She laid her head back and closed her eyes. A tear rolled out of each one.

Fernanda left the room, and, one by one, other nurses came in to look at Piedad, along with two cheerful nuns. All of them wanted to turn Piedad over on her stomach, but Piedad looked stonily at each one and closed her eyes.

The mother superior came back, this time worried.

"I'm afraid we won't have a doctor until morning," she said.

Piedad opened her eyes and glared at the nun. Madre Dolores smiled ruefully at me and glided out of the room, her white veil swirling a little over her shoulders.

I tried to remember what I had learned about burns in the first-aid course we had all been talked into taking during the war. Shock. With a hideous burn like Piedad's, the child ought to be in shock. I had never seen anyone in shock, but I had read descriptions. They didn't seem to fit Piedad at all.

Water. That I did remember. A new nurse came on duty: Caro, for Carolina. I asked her for a glass of water and a spoon.

"Yes," Caro said. "That's the best thing you can do."

Piedad was still on her back, so I could lift up her head to spoon a little water into her mouth. She drank thirstily and then threw up. Caro came running with one of the little curved throw-up dishes they have in hospitals.

"Didn't you bring a towel?" she asked me.

"No."

"Nor a blanket?"

"I didn't know I was supposed to," I said, apologetically.

Caro sighed deeply.

"You'll need a blanket," she said. "It's cold here at night. Is there anyone you can telephone?"

There was, and I did, and while I was spooning water and Piedad was throwing up, a friar arrived with a blanket for me and, better still, a Thermos of hot coffee.

Caro brought me a chair to sit on beside the bed. Supper came for the occupants of the other beds. The sun went down. Caro gave the last medicine, the last shots. The relations rolled up in their blankets and lay down beside or under the beds of their patients. Caro brought a carafe of water and put it on Piedad's bed table. Then she turned out the light and slipped out of the room. Still I spooned water into Piedad's thirsty little mouth, and still she threw up.

All night long we kept it up, Piedad and I, until, at 5:30 in the morning, Piedad drank a spoonful and it stayed down. She had successfully drunk nearly half the water in the carafe when, at seven o'clock, the doctor came in.

He was the first doctor to visit the hospital, and Piedad was the first patient he saw. He was a huge man, a bear of a man, with a likeable, stubby face and big, clever hands. Like so many big men, he was gentle. Piedad let him turn her over with no protest at all. When he saw the depth and the extent of the burn, his face darkened. From that time on, he was Piedad's doctor, and I was Piedad's slave.

Treatment began that morning and continued for the five months Piedad and I were together there in the hospital. Piedad disliked the I.V.'s and pulled out the needles, but she obligingly stayed on her stomach, and Fernanda found veins in Piedad's ankles that Piedad couldn't reach. Piedad spat out the gelatins and puddings of her prescribed soft diet and demanded tortillas and beans. The elegant hospital kitchen provided no such plebeian fare, but the nuns' kitchen did. The doctor, who came every morning, approved the change, and Madre Lucia, a dumpling of a nun, smuggled them in to me. I made small tacos of the beans and pieces of tortilla and popped them into Piedad's mouth. She chewed them seriously, methodically, until she finally said, "Enough."

We laid her with her head at the foot of the bed, where, lying on her stomach, she could look out at the whole room instead of at the wall. That way, too, I could kneel while Fernanda was tenderly bathing the great, ugly burn and swabbing on the burn medicine, and Piedad could hold my hands tightly, not to cry. The burn had started hurting after a little while.

She was such a tough, spunky little girl, it was impossible not to love her, and love her I did, as did almost everyone else who came to know her. She became the pet of the women's ward, the pet of the nuns, the nurses, the patients, and their attendants. She accepted our homage with great dignity and little response.

It took me no time at all to realize how lucky we were to be in the women's ward of a Mexican hospital. We were surrounded by friends to counsel, jolly, and console us. There must have been untold suffering in that room, but absolutely nobody complained. My respect for the poor of Mexico flowed over.

The woman in the first bed was old, with a sunken, toothless mouth and a glorious smile. There were always people with her, daughters, granddaughters, sons, and grandsons. The young men were even more affectionate with her than the women, smoothing back her hair, caressing her cheek, and holding her hand.

"How many children do you think I have?" she asked me, teasing. I guessed she had a dozen.

"No, twenty-one," she said.

"I would have had twenty-three," she said, as the women all laughed at my reaction. "Only my husband was sick for two years."

The woman in the bed next to Piedad's had a big family, too. She had ten children, and she was only thirty-one.

"The government is going to teach us not to have any more," she announced in her loud, clear voice. "The government doesn't want us to have more than we can support. It's all I can do to feed the ones I have; nothing but beans, and tortillas, and shrimp, shrimp, shrimp."

Her husband was a fisherman.

There was a woman across the aisle from us with a breast infection, a four-week-old baby, and a dark, fine-looking husband who never took off his new, cream-colored straw hat. The mother could sign her name, no more, but they were sending all their children through school. Their oldest son was already a certified public accountant. The baby was clean and pretty, and the nurses would pick it up and dance with it and threaten to steal it. The mother washed out its diapers, really embroidered table scarves, in our common lavatory, and the father hung them out to dry on the iron fence in front of the hospital.

On our second day, Fernanda helped me wash Piedad's hair, long, glossy black hair once we had cut away the burned frizz. I was terrified of leaving Piedad alone, but, while she was sleeping, I made a dash for the nearest native market, where I bought combs and barrettes in bright primitive colors. After we had washed and dried it, I coiled Piedad's hair on top of her head, holding it in place with all of the ornaments. Then I let her see, in my pocket mirror, how pretty she was. She did not smile.

She was a beautiful little girl. Her eyes were dark and slanting, her nose small and fine, her mouth mobile and expressive. When at last she did smile, her teeth were strong, even, and perfect.

Sometimes she cried. She would hold my hands tightly and beg.

"Let's go home," she would say. "Let's go home to Jesús María. Let's go home. Let's go home. Let's go home."

"But we're going, Piedad," I would tell her. "We're going just as soon as you're better. Why are you crying, Piedad?"

"*Es triste me corazon*," she would say. "My heart is sad."

The women in the ward tried to cheer her up.

"How pretty Piedad is," they would say. "What pretty eyes she has. So big."

Then the attendants would give her apples and tangerines, which she would eat seriously, methodically, without saying thank you.

One morning when Piedad was holding my hands while Fernanda gently swabbed her back, a Cora came stalking down the aisle between the beds, his head thrust forward, his arms slightly akimbo, obviously a young man spoiling for a fight.

Piedad saw him before I did.

"My father!" she called out, the first time I had heard delight in her voice.

I freed my hands and hurried down the aisle to meet him.

"I'm so glad you've come, Señor," I said.

He stalked past me without speaking, stopping only when he reached Piedad's bed. He looked on for a moment, and then all the fight went out of him.

"I came to take her home," he said. "But I can't, can I?"

"No," I said. "You can't, but you can have my chair."

From then on, he sat at the head of Piedad's bed, and they talked and talked in Cora, their heads close together, adoring each other. Piedad suddenly became a different little girl, twice as pretty, a bit naughty, obviously witty, as sometimes her father would laugh and laugh at something she said.

Everybody in the big, bright hospital room was happy. There with the smell of antiseptic and piney floor and alcohol, the sick were happy, their relations were happy, lovely Madre Dolores was happy, dumpy Madre Luisa, the other nuns, and the nurses were happy, and, next to Piedad, I was happiest of all.

Lucio, the father's name was. Lucio. He stayed with us for three whole days. The nuns let him sleep in the men's ward on the floor. Like all good Indians, he had his own blanket, neatly folded over the opening of his hand-woven woolen bag. Not only did he bring Piedad to life, but he gave me a little freedom as well.

The thing I was most terrified of, for Piedad, was infection, there in that room full of sick people with her raw burn exposed to the air. I wanted no one to touch her who was not as careful as I. Lucio was just as careful and more adroit. He was absolutely clean and so strong he could lift Piedad onto the bedpan with his two hands underneath her, not touching anywhere the edges of the burns that ran over her sides. He washed with soap the mango he brought her and then, almost gloating, watched her eat it up. He did not have the money to buy one for himself.

Before Lucio's appearance, my escapes from the hospital had

been few and furtive. I had gone to Tepic straight from the curato with nothing, not even a toothbrush. The second night in the hospital, I learned to sleep in my clothes, rolled up in my borrowed blanket. The nurses, all the time I was in the hospital, if there was one empty bed in the ward, saw to it that it was next to Piedad's. Only on the very rare occasions when all the beds were full did I have to sleep on the floor. All the same, at the start I did need clean underthings, toothpaste, cold cream, facial tissues, soap, and towels, one for Piedad and one for me. Toilet paper, too. I discovered that we were all supposed to supply our own. To get anything, I would wait until Piedad was asleep, and then I would dash out to the nearest store and then dash back again.

It was colder in Tepic than it had been in Jesús María, and I had only the dress I had worn to the curato. I couldn't leave the hospital long enough to get to a dress shop, and, for the first few days, I was not only grubby but also cold. Then another miracle did happen, like the one that had taken Padre Jacinto to Jesús María. My dear friend, she who had taught me to give a shot to an orange, appeared with her husband at the motel down the block.

I was having a cup of coffee in the restaurant, Piedad having regally given me permission to go. I was shivering. My friend saw me. She took off her own sweater and put it over my shoulders. Then she went back to her and her husband's room and returned with a plastic bag full of her own clothes. I went back to the hospital crying.

With Lucio there, I could do much more outside the hospital. I could look for fabric to make a pretty skirt for Piedad, whose own had burned off her back. I could buy her a doll that moved back and forth over a metate when you pulled a string. I could get a hot shower in the public baths the soccer players patronized, drying myself on my own towel. I could eat a real dinner at a Mexican restaurant where a waitress knew of my predicament and would run to bring me chicken, and rice, and coffee. And I could take a good meal back to Lucio, who refused to go outside to eat.

When he left, he asked me for three things: a snip of Piedad's fingernail, a strand of her hair, and a piece of her dress. She had no dress, but we cut a tiny swatch from her blanket and carefully folded all inside a sheet of facial tissue.

"For Don Teodulo?" I asked Lucio.

"No, another."

"Who?"

"Oh, just a curandero," he said. "Another."

I wasn't even going to learn the curandero's name. I told Lucio I hoped he would come back soon.

"I will," he said, "but Piedad is worried about her goat, and she is lonesome for her mother."

I knew she was. After Lucio left, I tried to reassure her.

"Your mother will come to see you," I said. "I'm sure she will come very soon."

Piedad looked me straight in the eye.

"Are you a liar?" she asked me.

Piedad's mother did come very soon; she was Petra, soft, dark, and officious. With her she brought the baby, Piedad's sulky seven-year-old sister, Eufrasia, who spoke no Spanish, a couple of bulging woven Cora bags, and one rather dirty embroidered bag full of tortillas. As soon as she had laid the tortillas out, side by side on the windowsill, she sat down by Piedad, ready to take command.

I would have been delighted to leave her in charge had she believed, as Lucio did, that there were unseen organisms that could cause infection.

Unfortunately, she did not.

In an effort to ward off the pneumonia that may attack anyone who is kept immobile in bed, I had devised a way of changing Piedad's position a little every hour or so. The burn had healed around the edges far enough so I could put a clean towel, tightly rolled, a little under one side of her ribs and then under the other. Petra couldn't understand why I didn't want her to put back the towel after it fell on the floor. She couldn't understand why I didn't want Piedad to eat the ice shaved from a dirty block on the street and flavored with colored syrup. She couldn't understand why she should wash her hands before lifting Piedad onto the bedpan or why, in so doing, she should be careful not to touch the edge of the burn. I continued to take care of Piedad, but Petra kept her happy.

She made a little home for herself at the side of Piedad's bed, a cozy corner where she could put the sleeping baby on her folded rebozo, a couple of blankets for herself and Eufrasia. She washed the rags that served as diapers in our common lavatory and hung them to dry on the slats under Piedad's bed. On one of my first excursions out of the hospital after her establishing residence there, I bought disposable paper diapers. Petra used them at first with suspicion and then with prodigality.

From the first moment she sat down at the head of Piedad's bed, she and Piedad, their heads close together, whispered and laughed, whispered and laughed, and always in Cora. I looked on, a foreigner, but a foreigner happy for a little Cora girl with a bad burn on her back—and only a trifle jealous.

On Saturdays, Lucio would appear, usually with his cousin Esteban, who, like Lucio, was working in the tobacco down on the coast. For two days, they would sit in a circle around the head of Piedad's bed, five of them: Petra, Lucio, Esteban, Eufrasia, and the baby. Piedad would make remarks in Cora, and everyone would laugh.

"Is she saying naughty things?" I would ask her mother.

"Very naughty," Petra would say and laugh again.

My Indian Village, the nuns and nurses called my family group and made no complaint. I wondered if there were any hospitals in the United States that would have tolerated it.

Eventually, I had to move Petra, and the baby, and sulky Eufrasia to the Franciscan hostel, as the baby caught a cold and was a peril to Piedad. But Petra came every morning with homemade tortillas and eggs cooked with onions, and tomatoes, and hot little chiles, and Piedad ate them hungrily and talked and laughed in Cora.

The baby, until it recovered, was banished to the far end of the room, away from the patients, poutingly attended by Eufrasia.

Piedad was improving. The doctor was reserved but seemed optimistic. The nuns and the nurses were pleased. I was certain that Piedad was really going to be well again. One day now, I could tell myself, I would be taking her home to her dark little house with the cozy smell of adobe and the soft dirt floor. Her baby goat would be bigger now, but it would still be hers, the baby goat her father had given her.

It was only a matter of time.

18

Requiem for Piedad

Piedad died at 6:25 on a Sunday morning in June.

The burn was almost well. There were only a few square inches that had not healed. She didn't die of the burn but of pneumonia. She died because she no longer had room in her lungs to breathe.

Nobody could have done more for her than the nuns, and the nurses, and the doctor himself.

The nuns had a square cloth tent made to shelter Piedad. It protected her from the contaminated air up to her coiffured head, which projected from an opening in the tent like a turtle's from its shell. The nuns contributed food, medicine, blood, and the operating room and anesthetist, along with incredible patience and constant encouragement.

The nurses not only cared for the burn and gave the shots and the I.V.'s (leaving me to watch the drip), but they also helped me wash Piedad's long, thick hair, helped me change her sheet without hurting her, and helped me cheer her up when neither of her parents was there to chat with her.

The doctor, big, burly, and infinitely gentle, never stopped trying. Skin grafting, which could have helped a smaller burn, was impossible for Piedad. She was lying on the skin that could have been used for grafting.

The local medication he started out with was working. The burn was contracting as the skin grew in from the edges, but he was eager for a better way. He asked if anyone in the States could find out for me if there were some new miracle treatment there, news of which had not reached Mexico.

I telephoned my daughter in Palo Alto, California. She told me to call her back in two days. I did. She had arranged for free treatment in the best burn center in California. She had arranged for free round-trip passage for Piedad and me on a U.S. airline. All I would need would be a visa for Piedad, a precisely worded, properly witnessed legal document, signed by both parents, giving me permission to take Piedad out of the country, and a bed built to exact specifications to fit in the plane.

The bishop passed through Tepic, stopped to see Piedad, and awarded me a Franciscan nun to take care of her while I dashed off to the U.S. consulate in Guadalajara.

I found out that I could not get a visa for Piedad without a passport. I could not get a passport for Piedad without her birth certificate. I dropped off to see the Huichol students in my house briefly, left them a little money to eat on, and dashed back to Tepic.

Lucio and Petra were both there. Lucio sent Petra with the baby and Eufrasia off to Jesús María, where Piedad's birth certificate was said to be filed in the Presidencia.

Padre Domingo appeared out of nowhere. He took Lucio with him to a lawyer for a paper that would permit me to take Piedad out of Mexico. The document had to be absolutely correct or it would be useless. I gave the padre the explicit directions my daughter had given me, written down. With a Mexican's inherent inability to accept directions from a woman, Padre Domingo returned with a document that fulfilled none of the requirements and left town.

Lucio went back to the coast to work in the tobacco.

Petra returned from Jesús María with the information that if Piedad's birth certificate actually was in the Presidencia, nobody could find it.

It was beginning to look as if Piedad and I were not meant to go to the burn center in California.

Meanwhile, in the hospital laboratory, the doctor was preparing little grafts of placenta, which, in some tests, had started skin growing in the middle of a burn. The nurses prepared Piedad and wheeled her to the operating room.

Lucio was in the women's ward with me when they wheeled Piedad back. She was still unconscious from the anesthetic. Lucio thought she was dying. He put his hat in front of his face and cried.

The placenta grafts did not take, but the area of the burn continued to diminish. Little by little, the backs of Piedad's legs, her armpits, and her crotch healed, and we could get Piedad out of bed. She and I would walk through the hospital with everyone smiling at us, for Piedad had become a personage with the ambulatory patients, as well as with the nuns and nurses. Sometimes we would walk in the garden, and Piedad would touch the roses. Her knees were bent from the scarring and her shoulders hunched over, but Piedad was on her feet and walking, and everyone was pleased.

Petra was almost always with us during the day, bringing Piedad her breakfast of homemade tortillas and Mexican eggs. Piedad's ill-natured little sister usually carried the baby slung in her own black rebozo, and Petra would make their little Cora snuggery at the head of Piedad's bed.

Sometimes, however, Petra would have to leave us for a few days, taking the children with her. Lucio's other wife was in the hut Piedad had shown me, tending the goats, the garden, and her own two children, but she was lazy, Petra said. She, Petra, had to fly out from Tepic every so often to make sure the second wife wasn't idling.

I hadn't known any Cora with two wives before; a couple of mestizos, yes, but no Coras. I asked Lucio.

"Not many," he said. "They haven't got enough money."

I remembered how insulted Piedad had been when I said her family was poor.

"Petra says your other wife is lazy," I said.

"She's young," Lucio said. "The truth is that Petra gets lonesome for her."

Both Lucio and Petra were in Jesús María during Holy Week. Lucio had to run with the Judíos, and Petra was one of the women charged with the duty of making tortillas from the corn that had been harvested in the fall from the communal cornfield on the mountain.

Madre Luisa, round and ruddy, smuggled tortillas and beans to Piedad while Petra was away, except on Good Friday, when the nuns were fasting. Piedad was cross all day. Madre Luisa also arrived in the women's ward every evening to lead the faithful in the Rosary. We would all kneel, those of us who were not in bed, while she, in a slow, commanding voice, intoned the Our Fathers and the Hail Marys and then waddled out, smiling over her shoulder at us, her obedient children.

The dramatis personae of the ward kept changing. We had all kinds of cases. One woman died. The rest got well and went home, making room for others.

Meanwhile, Piedad kept improving. The doctor operated again, this time grafting dime–size inserts from Piedad's arms into the center of the diminishing burn. They took. Little islands of new skin began to form in the middle of the burn that was left.

I was glad I had been unable to take Piedad to the burn center in California. There she would never have seen her parents. There would have been nobody there who spoke Cora, probably few who spoke Spanish. She might have been kept in isolation, I thought, and even I would have been permitted to see her only for a short period every day and possibly in a frightening white gown and cap and mask. The culture shock might have been as dangerous as the air–borne germs in the women's ward–and she was getting well.

The calendar came to have no meaning. Time rolled on only in relation to Piedad's improvement. The cold abated, and then warmth turned to heat. Sometime along the way, they began burning the cane fields preparatory to starting up the sugar mill. A light, white ash fell over Tepic, like snow. Every morning as I hurried to the cup of coffee Piedad graciously permitted me, a pretty lady in her pink wrapper, in front of her pink house, would be sweeping up the white ashes on the sidewalk between her two plots of pink roses.

After Holy Week, Petra stayed for a few days in the little thatched hut, and only Lucio came to Tepic, as strong and tender as ever. He sat as usual by Piedad's bed, talking to her confidentially in Cora. As usual, he was a great help to me. I could get a shower every day in the public baths patronized by the soccer players.

I could write long letters to my children.

I had arranged for Lucio to stay in the men's section of the Fran–ciscan hostel, and he usually left before the Rosary. One afternoon, however, we heard the little bell coming down the hall that signaled that a nun was heralding the approach of a priest on his way to give Communion to one or more of the patients. Lucio knelt with everyone else, but, after the priest had left, he sat back in his chair and began telling me about Holy Week, his eyes shining with mischief.

He had been running with the Judíos for eleven years, six past the required five. He told me how he made his mask of papiermâché, molding with his hands the muzzle, then the ears, to show me. He sketched with his fingers the deer antlers he had put on it to make it "more beautiful." As he outlined with his hand how he painted his body, he made a wicked face, eyes open wide, mouth pulled down. I asked him if he always painted his body the same way, and he said he did.

"Is that how I will know you next Holy Week?" I asked him.

"No," he replied, smiling. "I will lift up my mask and greet you."

I was sorry when Lucio left, but Petra soon returned with Eufrasia and the baby, and I was glad to see her. In spite of our differences, we had become fond of each other. Petra had come to tolerate my attitude toward germs as a harmless gringa aberration, and I had come to respect her attributes as a woman. Whether she was gossiping with Piedad, or embroidering on the floor, or nursing the baby, she was, first and last, a mother. She still frightened me sometimes. Now that the baby was old enough for solid food, Petra would feed her like a mother bird, chewing up something in her own mouth and then, with her fingers, transferring it to the baby's. Appalled as I was, I had to admit that I had never seen a healthier baby. After the cold in the head, she was never sick a day all the time we were in the hospital.

I was getting a little more tired all the time, as I always felt that I must wake up quickly if Piedad needed me in the night and seldom got enough rest. I was so hopeful, though, that it didn't really matter whether or not I slept. I figured that, within a month or two, we might be taking Piedad home.

Then she got pneumonia. After all the time that I thought she was out of danger, she got pneumonia.

The I.V.'s started up again, the shots in the little rump now cured of the burn, the capsules, the syrups, the orange juice. Madre Dolores, her beautiful, luminous eyes full of concern, came to sit beside her.

Piedad gave the madre her hand to hold. Madre Luisa intoned longer and longer prayers after the Rosary, kneeling by Piedad's bed.

"I want to take her home," Petra told me. "She's going to die. I want to take her home."

I refused.

"We will get her well," I insisted. "Have faith, Petra."

But Piedad didn't get well. Each day she got a little bit worse. There were x rays. They showed the functioning parts of her lungs getting smaller and smaller. I called up my friend in Guadalajara, the friend who had taught me to give shots. She tried her best to console me.

"There's always hope," she said.

But then, at 6:25 on a Sunday morning in June, Piedad stopped breathing and died. I was with her. I couldn't believe that she was dead. I went along with her when they took her on a stretcher and put her in a room I hadn't seen before, a room with tables in it. They put the stretcher on the table and left me with Piedad. My tough little, spunky little Indian. How could she be dead?

Petra came later with Eufrasia and the baby.

"I wanted to take her home," Petra said. "She should have died in the Sierra."

I telephoned the friar, who asked me if I wanted her buried in Tepic or in the mountains.

"In the mountains," I said.

The friar said that he would make all the arrangements and that Petra and I should go to the Franciscan warehouse.

I telephoned my friend in Guadalajara.

"I can't go to Jesús María tomorrow," she said in her matter-of-fact way, "but I'll be there on Tuesday."

I have never known what I ever did to have such a friend.

Petra and I, with Eufrasia and the baby, all went to the warehouse in a taxi. The friar had put a table in the middle of the big, windowless room with its sacks of corn and salt and sugar, its stacks of cotton blankets and cartons of medicines, all stored there for the missions. He had put out two chairs for us to sit on. Petra and Eufrasia sat on the floor, their backs against sacks of corn. I sat on one of the chairs, waiting.

It was afternoon when the friar brought Piedad's casket to the warehouse in the pickup truck. It was child size, white, and un-adorned. Piedad had been "prepared," as the friar said, so she didn't have to be buried at once. The friar struggled the casket onto the table, with help from Petra and me, and went to get candles from the little chapel attached to the warehouse. Eufrasia and the baby slept in Petra's blankets, piled on the floor, but Petra and I sat awake by the coffin all through the night.

Padre Jacinto arrived at the warehouse early Monday morning to fly us out. He and the friar wrestled the small coffin into the plane, and Petra and I sat on it. When we reached Jesús María, the padre buzzed it three times, so that when we touched down on the flats Fray Nicolas and the Cora named Gaspar were there to greet us.

"Where shall we take the box?" I asked Petra. "Have you relations here in town?"

"I thought we would take it to your house," Petra said. And so we did.

We pulled my Coca-Cola table into the room with the door on The Street of San Miguel, and the friar and Gaspar placed the box on it, open. I should have bought a fancy little white dress for Piedad and a crown of imitation pearls. A little girl must go to her grave looking like an angel as she lies in her coffin. Children must bring flowers to lay around her head. I had been too desolated to remember.

Piedad had no crown. She had no dress at all, only the gray blan-ket from the hospital up under her chin. People began to pour into my house as soon as we arrived, but we closed the coffin and opened it again only when a friend brought Lucio down from the mountains. Lucio looked, put his hat in front of his face to hide it, and disappeared.

Lucio's mother, the curandera, came.

"Why did you bring her here?" she angrily asked Petra. "Here to the house of the gringa?"

"She loved Piedad, too," Petra told her. "You should have seen her. She couldn't stop crying."

Fray Nicolas arrived with the big brass candlesticks the Coras had in church, and I sent a boy to Don Serafim for the candles he made with wax from his bees. The bishop and Padre Domingo were both away, so there could be no Mass. The hearty nun from equatorial Africa had left in May, overcome by the heat, but there were new nuns in the curato, Franciscan nuns. They came, two of my old friends from Santa Clara, Madre Maria and Madre Cristina. They knelt on my dusty brick floor to recite a Rosary, and all who were in the house, most of them sitting on the floor, went on their knees to join in.

Lucio returned, calm and confident. He had found a Huichol who had peyote. He had bought five buttons and had eaten them. He was in complete control of himself and everyone else.

Chela came and cried. Lucio's cousin Esteban came with two slats of wood nailed together to make a small cross. I had a felt-tipped pen, and with it I printed Piedad's name on the crosspiece and the date of her death down below. Nobody knew exactly in what year she had been born. Indians keep no track of trivialities.

The house filled up, mostly with Coras but with mestizos, too. Chela brought a great stack of tortillas.

I knew that most of the guests were going to stay the night, but at midnight I collapsed. I said good-night and went to get a few hours sleep on a cot Chela had loaned me to put in my storeroom across the patio. Before the sun was up, Lucio was shaking me.

"We must go to the holy field," he said. The burying ground. I got up.

"We need alcohol," he said. "Drinkable alcohol, also Pepsi Cola."

I had potable alcohol I used for making scorpion drops. Lucio had apparently bought Pepsi Cola the day before.

"We only need two now," he said, pouring some Pepsi from each bottle into a glass he had found in my house. "We'll need the others later."

Then he filled the Pepsi bottles with alcohol while I looked on, blinking, and we set off, the two of us in the early dawn, up the switchback and over the mountain to the burying ground on the other side. Two gravediggers were there, having apparently finished their task. The sun was just coming up. Lucio asked me to examine the hole. Was it wide enough, long enough, deep enough? I thought it was, and Lucio gave the gravediggers the bottles, each with enough alcohol to stun them, I thought.

Then Lucio and I went up over the mountain and down the trail to the switchback. Suddenly, Lucio touched my arm and stopped, motionless. A little deer had leapt across our path, not twenty feet in front of us. Lucio stood looking at the brush at the side of the trail into which the deer had disappeared.

"I have never in my life seen a deer so close before," he whispered. "And I am sure nobody has ever seen one here, so close to Jesús María."

The pallbearers were waiting when we got back to my house. Lucio prepared some more bottles of Pepsi and alcohol. Esteban picked up the cross, and we started once more up the switchback and over the mountain. Petra had a tin cup of water and a posy of flowers with her, to sprinkle water on the coffin after it was lowered into the ground. Esteban carefully pushed the point of the cross into the earth after the coffin was covered. The pallbearers drank their Pepsi and alcohol, and we all started home.

As we came to the place where the little deer had crossed our path, Lucio looked sharply at the thicket where the deer had disappeared.

In the magic world of the Indian, the deer holds a special place. Why, on that day of all days, had one appeared there, right before us? What did it mean to Lucio? A message from his daughter? An assurance from his God?

Lucio had never seen a deer so close before—and he was sure that nobody had ever seen a deer so close to Jesús María.

19

Two Brides, Both in White

After a couple of weeks away, I was back in Jesús María. It was late June, and the rains had not yet started. The air was parched; the sun, scorching. The river grumbled along, brown and sluggish. The scorpions were still hiding under the rocks. There was, however, interesting news. There were going to be two weddings in Jesús María, both in the church.

While I was with Piedad, Jaime, the veterinarian, had finally broken down Arcelia's resistance and, with her permission, had formally proposed to Luz. Luz had accepted him. Since she had treated him with civility but apparent indifference for more than a year, interested spectators were more than a little surprised. Chela alleged, however, that in the end she had capitulated gracefully.

"She sat down as soon as he began to propose," she said, "so that she could look up at him instead of down."

Preparations for the wedding were being made, but in Guadalajara. All the hullabaloo here in Jesús María was over another marriage, that of my friend Chuy.

She had been living at home on the rancho since the nuns had taken over the work of the curato, but her father, Don Mariano, came into town every week or so. I met him on The Street in Front of the Church the first day I was back in Jesús María.

"Come to the wedding and eat meat," he said. "I'm going to kill a cow."

It had a familiar ring. Don Basilio had said the same thing when he invited me to the wedding up at El Cerro. "I'm going to kill a cow."

There was a difference, though: Don Mariano was a Cora; it was his daughter who was going to be married, not his son; and the wedding was actually going to be in church.

During the time that I had been in Jesús María, there had never been another Cora wedding with benefit of clergy. All the Cora marriages had been more or less like that of Lucio's young cousin Esteban.

Esteban was a handsome youth who almost always had a pleased smile on his guileless face. One day he came into the crumbling little room into which Madre Maria had moved the medicine, looking more than usually radiant. After a few minutes of pleasantries, he burst out with his news.

"I have a wife," he said, his eyes wide with the wonder of it.

"Really!" I said. "Is she hard working?" It was the most important question where women have so much work to do.

"Oh, yes."

"Does she make good tortillas?"

"Does she not!"

"Is she clever at weaving?"

He showed me his hand-woven bag of blue and green yarn. It was a beauty.

"Were you married in the Presidencia, Esteban?"

I knew, of course, that he had not been married in church.

He looked at me with something like pity.

"No," he said, "not the Presidencia."

"Did your fathers agree that you should marry?"

"We have no fathers."

"Your mothers, then?"

Esteban could scarcely contain his elation. "They gave her to me," he said, hugging himself.

For Chuy, marriage was going to be different. I assumed that Don Mariano had agreed with the father of Armando, Chuy's young man, that the marriage was a good one, but the wedding was actually going to be Catholic. Everybody was excited, especially Chela.

"She's my goddaughter," Chela said with a proprietary smile. "I taught her her catechism when she was a little girl. She hasn't forgotten."

Chela had already started a wedding dress for Chuy. It was a modest dress of white poplin with long sleeves and a big, round collar. Chela trimmed the collar and the cuffs with lace she had saved for herself. She fitted Chuy with a pair of white shoes from the store. She had ordered white tulle from Tepic for Chuy's veil.

Chuy came in from the rancho and stood docilely while Chela fitted the dress. It was, indeed, a very plain dress for a church wedding in Jesús María, but Chuy did look stunning in white, and the other preparations were worthy of Chela at her most exuberant.

She picked the damas for Chuy, the bridesmaids. She decreed that they should wear the rose–colored dresses they had worn at a previous wedding. She put all the damas to work making paper flowers to string in garlands from the high chandelier to the spikes in the walls of the church. She showed them how to make gladiolas to fill the big urns on either side of the altar. She herself made roses of pink facial tissue to go on the altar in fruit–juice cans.

Chuy came in to watch only occasionally. Don Mariano's rancho was over the river and far away. In the flurry of busy mestiza girls, she looked more Cora then ever, with her lustrous dark skin, her shiny black hair, and her colored basque and wildly flowered skirt. She looked on with her almond eyes, disbelieving and, I thought, just a little amused. Once, when I too was in the sala, she gave me a distinctly wicked smile.

Padre Domingo was in Tepic. Don Mariano asked the sixth–grade teacher to write a note to him asking him to come back to Jesús María for the wedding. Don Mariano signed it with his thumb.

"I would have liked it to be the bishop," Chuy whispered to me, "but he's not here. People say that wherever he is, it's very far away."

She was right. He was in Rome.

Every time Don Mariano came into Madre Maria's little clinic, he said it again.

"Come to the wedding and eat meat. I'm going to kill a cow."

All of the brides who had been married in church since I had been in Jesús María had been mestizas. I couldn't remember that any of them had been married in white. The fathers of the girls in Jesús María were very strict. They would not permit young suitors to enter the house. The result, Don Serafim told me, was that young lovers met at the river. Then, in the natural course of events, the girl went to live with the boy, usually at his parents' house. Sometimes they went through a civil service in the Presidencia, sometimes not. Always, the girl's family refused to recognize her until the nuptial Mass was celebrated. Sometimes the young couple had a baby or two before that transpired.

Sometimes the delay was for economic reasons. The mestizo groom had to buy the bride's wedding dress, her veil, her shoes. That took money. His father had to provide the banquet after the wedding. That took money, too. Only when enough money was on hand would the church bells ring and the bride appear at the door of the church, exquisite in a confection of pink, blue, yellow, or pale green, sometimes with a train, always with a billowing tulle veil, and often with many attendants. Then the padre or the bishop would walk solemnly up the aisle, possibly scold the bride a little in a low voice, and then bless the wedding party and precede them down the aisle to the altar.

So it was going to be with Chuy, except that she was going to the altar as a señorita, in white, and it was not Armando's father but her own who was going to kill the cow.

Padre Domingo flew into El Cerro on the morning of the wedding. The Datsun's front axle was cracked, so he hiked down to Jesús María, hugged the children who came running to meet him, and confessed Chuy, Armando, Armando's best man, all the bridesmaids, and Chela, who was to be matron of honor in the wedding. Then, after changing into their long, rose-colored dresses, all the bridesmaids congregated in Chela's living room.

Chuy was already there, squirming into her modest white wedding dress. Chela was waiting in her tight pink one, now in the role of beautician. After torturing the hair of all the girls into improbable puffs, dips, and curls, Chela started on Chuy's face. She made it up with green eye shadow, black eye liner, scarlet lipstick, and a foundation quite a little lighter than Chuy's own complexion. To Chela, dark skin was ugly, even when it was glossy and fine like Chuy's.

The bridesmaids put on their rose–colored crowns of artificial flowers. Chela attached Chuy's white tulle veil with bobby pins so the magnificent edifice of hair on top of her head would be fully visible and pressed a small bouquet of white artificial flowers into her hands, and we all headed for church.

The wedding was a pretty one. Padre Domingo was as delighted as Chela to have a Cora wedding in the church, and he radiated satisfaction. The bridesmaids were all mestiza girls who already knew the drill: when to take the bouquet away from the bride, when to present the coins, how to drape the white–beflowered lasso around the shoulders of the bride and groom without disturbing Chuy's veil.

Chuy's young man, Armando, was a handsome, dusky youth with a strong chin, a good mouth, and a determined look in his eye. He came from a rancho on the other side of the mountain, and I had seen him only once before.

Chuy looked radiant in her plain white dress and, yes, submissive. When she promised to obey, I almost believed that she would.

After the wedding, the ceremonial embraces in front of the church, and the photographs, we all trudged up the rock–paved road to the wedding banquet, all except Padre Domingo, who hiked off to San Francisco to celebrate Mass.

Don Mariano's own house was so far away that the wedding banquet was at his sister's house, one of the few Cora houses up in the mestizo part of town. The house was surrounded by the usual stone wall, just high enough to keep out the pigs and with no gate. Chuy and the bridesmaids, with the agility of youth, climbed over it gracefully. I clambered over behind them, skinning an ankle.

The table was set on one side of a small courtyard, under a shelter made of saplings and blankets. Behind the table, a white sheet hung down from the flannel roof, with flowers pinned to it and postcards. The bridesmaids and I were firmly directed to sit down at the table.

Chuy, her father and silent mother, Armando and his parents, Chela and the best man were ushered into a room off the courtyard, where they stayed for half an hour while we waited. Chela told me about it later.

"There were blankets on the floor," she said, "and a candle for each of us. Mariano lighted the candles, and we all knelt down on the blankets. Chuy's and Armando's parents began to pray, all together, in Cora. As they were praying, they all began to cry. Then Chuy and Armando began to cry, and pretty soon the best man and I were cry-

ing, too. Nobody had a handkerchief. Chuy's mother was blowing her
nose on her rebozo, and the men were blowing theirs on the floor. I
had some facial tissues, so I gave a couple to Chuy and kept a couple
for myself."

"Do you suppose that, to the Coras, that was the real wedding,
Chela?" I asked her.

"The marriage in the church was the real marriage," Chela replied
primly. "But sometimes the Coras are dear, aren't they?"

The banquet was a great success. Don Mariano's cow must have
been pampered, because the meat was very tender. The tortillas were
fresh, warm, and moist. To drink we had a choice of Pepsi, Coke, or
Fanta. Mestiza girls, as well as Coritas, served the plates and kept
bringing more tortillas to the table, hot from the griddle. There was a
wedding cake, only one layer but lavishly decorated. Doña Estela,
who made hot buns to sell, had given it to Chuy. Everyone was happy
about having Coras married in the church, everyone loved Chuy today, and everyone wanted to help.

That evening, I dropped into Chela's store. Armando was buying
groceries. He was still wearing his tight, navy-blue wedding trousers
and his white wedding shirt. He was also wearing a big white hat, a
very becoming one. It had a wide, roman-striped band with ribbons
hanging down the back. He was filling a small carton with food.

"They're going on their honeymoon," Chela told me from behind
the counter. "To San Francisco." Chuy grinned at me.

It sounded like going from the Bronx to Brooklyn. It was enterprising, though. Most couples just went home to the groom's mother.

I saw them crossing the river the next morning. Armando, still in
his wedding finery and with the wide ribbons fluttering down from
the back of his big white hat, was sitting proudly on a mule, the carton of groceries under his arm. Chuy was following in her new yellow
dress, picking her way delicately over the stones with her clever bare
feet, her shiny new black shoes in her hand.

I saw Don Mariano a few days later.

"That was a fine wedding," I told him, "and the beef was delicious."

"Well," he said, "of course they're going to have a baby, but the
girl wanted to get married in church, so what could I say? 'Go ahead,'
I said. 'Go ahead and have your wedding, and I'll kill a cow.'"

I hoped that when the baby was born, Chela would not count on her fingers. I knew how distressed she would be. Chuy! Her god-daughter! To whom she had taught her catechism!

Chela was so triumphant over Chuy's wedding that she could ig-nore the fact that she had absolutely nothing to do with Luz's. As was correct, that wedding was entirely in the hands of the groom and his somewhat startled family. Preparations had started before the Cora nuptials.

Jaime flew to Tepic on the way to Guadalajara. Arcelia let Luz ac-company him up to El Cerro with José. Don Basilio told me later that, before boarding the plane, Jaime had kissed Luz only on the cheek but had held onto her hand quite a lot longer than necessary. Don Basilio said Luz looked embarrassed but pleased.

Jaime came back within the week, and two weeks later his family flew in. They had come on a special flight straight from Guadalajara with a pilot bold enough to land on the now-hazardous airstrip down on the flats.

I heard the plane as it buzzed the town before landing and slipped out of the curato to see who had come. On the ledge behind the church, there was already a row of men in their big white hats and women in their speckled black rebozos peering down at the Beechcraft. I joined them.

Jaime was there with José and the pickup truck, now repaired. The pilot got out of the plane first, opened the cargo compartment, and began unloading. Jaime helped the passengers, apparently unac-customed to small planes, to alight. There were two women in city dresses and three men, unbelievably in jackets and ties. "*Ricos*," breathed the woman next to me. "Rich people."

The pilot and José were piling cartons, and bags, and boxes, and suitcases from the plane into the back of the pickup truck. The two women each took a large box from the pilot. Even from the ledge, we could see that the boxes, of transparent plastic, were full of flowers.

The pilot climbed back into the plane, pirouetted on the sandy airstrip, and took off with a great rooster tail of dust behind. Jaime and his family climbed into the truck—the ladies in the front seat with José, the men behind with the luggage—and headed for the new gov-

ernment building, where Jaime worked and lived. The spectators on
the ledge dispersed, and I went into the curato to pick up streptomycin for a young Cora father with TB who lived downriver.

After a shot in the young man's well-punctured rump, I stopped
by the government building to pay my respects to the visitors. Jaime
had an apartment there with a modern kitchen, the only one in Jesús
María. It had a stove and a refrigerator, both running on tank gas. It
also had four rooms with cots in them for visiting dignitaries, so he
could easily bed down his family. He introduced me to them: his
mother, a sister, his father, and two brothers. They all stopped un-
packing to greet me cordially.

The women were in the kitchen, storing food from the cartons in
the refrigerator and then removing it to make room for flowers. There
was an elaborate wedding bouquet of white roses and baby's breath
in a transparent plastic box, still dewy inside. Another huge one was
full of white gladiolas, for which the ladies requested buckets of water. Another smaller one, of white cardboard, they tucked with the
wedding bouquet in the refrigerator. On the table was a towering box
from a caterer, which I surmised carried the cake.

There were several enormous suit boxes in the other room, from
an elegant boutique that specialized in everything for glamorous
brides and fifteen-year-olds. The men were in their shirtsleeves, having sensibly removed their ties and jackets. As soon as they had unpacked their own suitcases, they went outside looking for a cool place
to sit down but not finding one. Jaime filled two buckets with precious water from the barrel outside, water provided to flush the toilet
in the bathroom. The ladies carefully arranged the gladiolas in the
buckets and professed their eagerness to meet their prospective
relatives-to-be.

With Jaime and his mother in the lead, we trooped up to Arcelia's
house under the blazing sun of the early afternoon. Jaime's father
and brothers had unbuttoned their shirts almost to their belt buckles,
but his mother and sister were still in their hot city dresses. Worse
still, they were wearing their delicate city shoes and teetered pain-
fully over the cruel rocks of the road. I could tell, from their silence,
that they were seeing the cocoa-colored street and the pigs as I had

seen them when I first trudged up the street beside the bishop. Nothing Jaime had told them could possibly have prepared them for Jesús María.

Arcelia and Luz were waiting, both prettily dressed but obviously nervous. Jaime's family crowded into Arcelia's poor little house with its makeshift counter and, with the courtesy that seems endemic with Mexicans, presented themselves charmingly to Arcelia, embraced Luz affectionately, and looked for a place to sit down. There were the two rickety chairs and the barrel. Chela appeared at the door.

We filed across The Street of San Miguel after Chela to climb up the steps to her store, to stoop along the narrow aisle with huaraches hanging at eye level, and finally to seat ourselves in her parlor with its plastic-covered sofa and chairs, its holy pictures, and knickknacks. Chela was at her most ingratiating, offering lemonade, store cookies, and lodging. Jaime's family gratefully accepted the refreshments but graciously declined the rooms, as they had their own beds with Jaime. Jaime's mother and sister did buy huaraches from Chela on their way out, considerably more practical than the thin-soled slippers they were wearing.

The wedding was only two days away. Jaime and his family left us to go to the curato, there to meet the bishop. He had already given Luz and Jaime their premarital instructions and, I was sure, would receive the Guadalajara family with his usual benevolence.

The next day, the women of Jaime's family set to work in earnest. They examined the church, astonished at the elegance of the santitos in the niches in the wall up behind the two altars, bemused by the garlands of flowers swooping down from the chandelier to the spikes in the wall. They had been left there after Chuy's wedding to serve for Luz's. I was afraid that Jaime's mother and sister would want to take them down as being entirely too countrified, but, their good manners showing, the ladies gracefully left them where they were.

The sheaves of white gladiolas made a handsome display in the aged gray urns in front of the new altar, and the women tied small sprays of the same white flowers with white satin ribbon to the ends of the backs of the pews. The red strip of carpet would not lead from the door to the altar until just before the wedding.

After they had finished with the church, Jaime's women picked up Luz and her damas, who were waiting at Chela's, along with two little boys and a little girl Luz had picked for her attendants. All of them trooped down to the government building to try on the creations from the Guadalajara boutique.

The wedding the next day was spectacular. Owing to the chivalry of the groom and the vigilance of the bride's mother, Luz's wedding gown was white. And what a gown! High necked and long sleeved, it had a "V" of ancestral lace on the bodice and a train that reached at least two meters out to the two little boys manfully trying to keep it off the red carpet. In deference to her height and Jaime's, Luz's long veil billowed out from a wreath of white roses flat on her smooth, shiny hair, and her white satin slippers had no heels.

Having neither father nor uncles, Luz had asked Don Paco to give her away. Alongside his impressive height, Luz looked positively delicate—and radiant. I had never seen her so pretty before.

Jaime, waiting at the altar, looked perfectly calm and, surprisingly, amused. He had fought a good, clean fight and had won.

The wedding dinner was quite properly in the government building. Jaime's family was firmly in charge. Only the wedding party, members of Arcelia and Chela's family, and I were invited, but we were still a throng.

Jaime's father and brothers had put tables together under the cement roof of an outdoor passageway, and out of those boxes from Guadalajara had come lace tablecloths. Somehow the women had conjured up a feast (I think they worked all night), and Jaime had engaged six Cora girls to serve it. It was a very merry party, with all the damas in their beautiful sea-green dresses, Chela flirting with Jaime's father, and Luz and Jaime managing to look like a contented, long-married couple.

Only Arcelia did not take part in the gaiety. As custom demanded, she had sat through the entire nuptial Mass looking glum. She did break with tradition by attending the dinner afterward, but she observed the proprieties by looking stonily into the distance, eating little, and speaking to no one. I felt sorry for her, usually so comfortable and charming, now in an expensive dress of Chela's that was too loose for her, and her hair tortured by Chela into an improbable French roll. She scarcely even glanced at the lofty wedding cake, with its scrolls of icing, when the Cora girls set it before Luz and Jaime.

The Guadalajara contingent continued gracious and urbane, but they couldn't help eyeing their new in-laws with some wonderment. I saw Jaime's mother startle the first time she saw Chela, in her modish dress from Guadalajara, grabbing a chunk of chicken in a torn-off piece of tortilla and opening her mouth wide to stuff the bundle into her cheek to chew.

The plane came back for Jaime's family the next day, and the newly married couple squeezed in with them, to go on from Guadalajara to Mexico City for their honeymoon. Luz climbed into the plane with considerably more grace than the other women. After all, she had flown in a little airplane twice before, once to Tepic on her way to Chihuahua and once on the way home.

I left Jesús María before Luz and Jaime returned and took off for a long-delayed visit with various members of my family in the States. When I came back, I found Luz temporarily staying with her mother. Jaime was off in the mountains, visiting ranchos, and Luz was timorous about staying alone in the modern apartment there in the government building. I found her in the room with the homemade counter, studying. She was sitting on one of the shaky chairs, with her book in her lap, her notebook and pencil on the barrel. She looked up at me and smiled.

"My husband the doctor says I must finish school, but," she said benignly, "you won't have to worry about me any more. My husband the doctor is paying my tuition."

Correct to the last, Jaime, cheerful and competent, saw to it that Luz graduated at the head of her class and had her first baby a full twelve months after the wedding.

20

And We Thought She Rode So Well

The day the horse threw me, I had my choice: I could ride an ugly, lazy, neurotic brute down to Jesús María or I could walk. The Datsun was there in El Cerro, but José was in Tepic with the keys. I elected not to walk. I had walked before.

That other time, there was not only no wheeled transport but no mount, either. Disregarding the concern of Don Basilio and Doña Dora, I had left my bags and boxes with them, had slung my camera strap over my shoulder, and had started off down the road singing the Anvil Chorus.

The road, with its rocks, and ruts, and potholes, was mean enough in crepe-soled shoes. In city shoes, it was murder. The sun was blistering. The road kept getting steeper on the upswings and rockier going down. The camera got heavier and heavier. By the time I reached Aurelia's house, the only one on the road, I was limping. By the time I reached the halfway mark, the gigantic wild fig, I was beginning to whimper.

From the tree, the road climbed yet another mountain before it finally settled down to the bridge. There was a shortcut, however. It was over a field of football-size rocks alongside the river. After what seemed like a mile of rocks, one arrived at a ford. On the far side of the ford was the upriver end of Jesús María.

I managed to work my way through the rocks in my city shoes, only occasionally twisting my ankle, until I came to the ford. I did not feel clever enough to cross it, as it was more than knee deep and was paved with boulders. I was afraid of wetting my camera. I started picking my way back to the wild fig.

At the prospect of climbing up and over another mountain, I had stopped whimpering and started to cry. Then I heard a voice calling from across the river, "Doña Cata! Doña Cata!" A man there was frantically signaling me to go back to the ford. I pointed to my camera, and he pointed up the bluff. An austere elderly gentleman was riding along the road on a very fine mule.

A little boy rode the mule across the river. I climbed into the saddle and freed a stirrup so the little boy could climb up behind me. We crossed without even getting our feet wet, and everybody was happy except for the elderly gentleman, who mounted his mule without comment and rode austerely on.

Perhaps if I had not remembered so vividly the despair I had felt on that miserable five-mile trek, I would not have accepted so readily the horse Don Basilio offered me. I hated it before I even mounted it, and I think it hated me. It was a clumsy oaf of a horse, and it looked at me with its head askew and the whites of its eyes showing. It was so tall that Don Basilio had to lead it to a rock so I could climb aboard. Out of deference to the bishop and respect for the heat, I was not wearing slacks. Mounting in a skirt was awkward, but it was a wide skirt, and I managed to accommodate myself in the saddle with a fair degree of modesty. I was leaving my suitcase and cartons in Don Basilio's storeroom as before, but Don Basilio tied my Cora bag on the pommel of the saddle and my sleeping bag on behind me as he gave me the usual parting wish that all would go well with me.

I thanked him and kicked the horse. It bridled a little, shook its head, stamped once, and stood still. Don Basilio gave it a resounding thump on the rump, and it reluctantly started down the road.

There was a small shrub on the right, a little higher than the weeds. The horse eyed it and shied to the left. There was a little shrub on the left. The horse shied to the right. I straightened it out and kicked it, and it moved sullenly ahead for perhaps a city block before it shied again.

The stirrups were inches too short, and one was shorter than the other. The horse poked along, no matter how hard I kicked it, and I didn't dare dismount to break a switch off a tree because the horse was so tall I wasn't sure I could mount again. Anyway, there were very few trees.

The sun was merciless. I had no hat. The road seemed endless. My kicking leg got very tired.

At last we reached the wild fig at the river, and I took again the shortcut over the stones. The horse, slipping and stumbling, picked out special ones to startle at. When we came to the ford, the horse crossed the river like an old lady with bifocals, head down, eyeing the boulders under the water, and still slipping and stumbling.

At last we blundered into the atrium, shying at the gate. There was a Cora in the atrium, and four more seated on the stone bench on the covered sidewalk of the ancient building across the road. They all regarded me impassively as I started to dismount.

When getting off a psychotic horse, it is wise to have someone at the horse's head, holding the bridle. I was provoked past wisdom. I endeavored to dismount without help and got my right leg stuck on my sleeping bag. I had forgotten it was tied on behind the saddle. The horse went crazy and began to buck.

"Grab the bridle!" I yelled to the Cora in the atrium.

He approached the horse tentatively, and the horse reared. The Cora quickly retreated. Somehow I managed to get my leg over the sleeping bag and to grab the cantle of the saddle. I was already hanging on to the pommel. The horse began to rear, but everything was going to be all right, rearing or no, if I could just get my left foot out of the stirrup.

But then the horse decided to whirl. On the third or fourth whirl, it flung me off to land hard on my side some ten feet away.

The Coras on the bench looked on with mild interest. The Cora in the atrium just stood. I wiggled my toes and fingers, decided my back was not broken, and tried to get up. I couldn't. At least, in the whirling, my foot had come out of the stirrup. I could be glad of that. Being dragged by a horse can lead to a very dirty death.

The horse, having got rid of me, stood sullenly. The Cora stood blandly. I sat helplessly. Finally, I ordered the Cora to grab the reins, hammer on the burros' door into the curato, and then unsaddle and tether the horse.

Madre Maria and the Cora Gaspar came running out to my assistance. They hauled me up and half carried me into the curato. After tethering and unsaddling the horse, the Cora detached my Cora bag and my sleeping bag and dumped them both at the gate.

For the next three weeks, I was a guest of the Franciscans.

I could not have arrived disabled at a more inconvenient time. The bishop was going to return from his trip to Rome. Padre Do– mingo had gone to meet him in Guadalajara. The madres, indeed all the mestizas of the town, were engaged in elaborate preparations to welcome the bishop home. Madre Maria was drilling the girls in new songs to sing. Madre Cristina was overseeing the making of yards and yards of paper lace and hundreds of paper flowers. Fray Nicolas was busy, too. From my bed, I couldn't make out exactly what he was doing, but I heard the boys' choir shouting out new songs of their own to sing.

Madre Maria had deposited me in her new little clinic while she made the bed in the room they always said was mine. It was a stan– dard Franciscan bed, planks on trestles, but Madre Maria laid on top what they call a mattress in the Sierra. (We gringas would call it a quilt.) Then she put on two short sheets, lovingly embroidered down the side in the Mexican way, and a light blanket, for, hot as the days were, the nights could turn cool toward morning.

With my arms around the shoulders of Madre Maria and Gaspar, I hopped and hobbled into the bedroom and cautiously lowered my– self onto the bed. I was sure my leg was broken.

The next few days are best forgotten. Madre Maria gave me shots for pain when I asked for them and brought me food three times a day. I found I could walk, hanging onto walls and limbs of trees, so I was spared the ignominy of a bedpan. I could even bathe in the crude concrete shower. The water was cold, but it was wet, and it felt good to be clean. Getting into my clothes required ingenuity, espe– cially into my shoes and stockings, but I managed.

I knew I probably ought to get to a doctor in Tepic or Guadala– jara, but I couldn't possibly climb into the pickup, and the jolting ride to the airstrip was clearly contraindicated. If Chela had been there, she would have had a stretcher made for me, but Chela was in Guadalajara on a buying trip, preparing for the customers who would swarm into town to honor the bishop. There was nothing for me to do but to stay in the curato until I was fit to travel, making as little of a nuisance of myself as I could.

My leg, from hip to knee, was an abstract painting in livid tones of yellow, red, navy blue, green, and deep, rich purple. I decided I ought to show it to our current doctor-to-be. I hobbled over to the Health Center and lifted my skirt. The doctor looked at my leg and roared with laughter. I had thought he might like to examine me, but, since he showed no intention of doing so, I dropped my skirt and hobbled back to the curato.

The hurting in my leg began to subside a little, and I found that one of the curato's few chairs was no more uncomfortable than my spartan bed, so I began working in what was now Madre Maria's clinic. There I sat, in the small, crumbling room, and pointed to medicines on the shelf for the patients to reach down, until I got swept into the frantic manufacture of paper lace.

It was a kindergarten exercise and just what a lame lady from New York needed to keep her mind off her leg. Every pair of scissors in Jesús María was cutting paper. Arcelia's gave her an enormous blister on the inside of her thumb as testimony to valor. I took the best care I could of it and put on a soft bandage to reduce the abrasion as Arcelia kept right on cutting. I myself had a pair of very good scissors hidden away in the carton of sterile gauze squares, so I could cut my share.

The object was to make streamers of colored tissue paper about six inches wide, scalloped on the bottom, and with cutout openwork of hearts, cloverleafs, diamonds, or whatever the cutter fancied. To accomplish this involved folding big squares of tissue paper over and over and cutting through several thicknesses so the design would repeat. I wasn't sure how the streamers were to be used, but I kept right on cutting.

I limped up to Arcelia's house, to keep out of the way in the curato, and joined the paper-lace party there. We cut in the daytime and pasted at night—Arcelia, Juana, Inez's Luz, and I. Usually, a man or two would join us in the evening. Sometimes Jaime's Luz would be there, studying, and she would explain that her husband the doctor had had to ride out into the mountains. Every evening, Juana made paste of flour and water. Everyone agreed it was better than boughten glue.

We pasted the strips together, end to end, to make long, long swags. Then we pasted the upper side of the swags over a heavy cord and carefully hung the finished festoons over a door to dry.

Chela came home a couple of days before the bishop. She rode down Pullman in the seat of the Datsun, as José had returned from Tepic some days before. The back of the pickup was piled with cartons full of merchandise. Arcelia, Juana, and Inez's Luz ran out to help unload the cargo, and José cheerfully got out from behind the wheel and carried the booty into the store. I limped across the street from Arcelia's house to see the fun.

Chela was resplendent in her city clothes, a bright turquoise suit with wide pants and white shoes with platform soles. There was no room for all her cartons in the narrow little store, so the women piled them on the floor of the sala, the living room. Chela went down on her knees and frantically began cutting the cords that tied them with a big knife Don Paco kept in the store.

"Paco's bringing the rest," Chela panted, as she struggled to open a carton. "We owe everyone in Guadalajara," she said with a laugh. "We bought out the town."

Arcelia, Juana, and Inez's Luz were lifting things out of the cartons to see what Chela had bought: plastic sandals in white, pink, blue, and lavender; black lace mananitas; speckled black jersey rebozos; lengths of percale in bright red, bright green, bright orange, bright blue; filigree earrings in make–believe gold; baby–size crosses; hand cream; toothpaste; white christening dresses for little girls; white christening suits for little boys; brightly printed kerchiefs for men.

Customers began to drift in. They sidled down the narrow aisle of the store, ducking under the huaraches hanging from above.

"Come in, come in," Chela called, and she began to sell on her knees, straight from the boxes.

A Cora I didn't know helped me back to Arcelia's to start cutting paper lace again. Don Paco eventually arrived, in the second trip of the Datsun. I had walked enough. I took his load on faith. He would have brought coils of rope, plastic pails of many colors, powdered milk, kerosene, flashlight batteries, and a dozen cases of Pepsi.

As the day of the bishop's arrival got nearer, I discovered what I had been making paper lace for. It was to make swags from the crown of the church to the poles now planted in the atrium and over the path the bishop would take from the airstrip down on the flats up to the gate of the atrium. Just about every able-bodied man in Jesús María, Cora and mestizo alike, was out digging holes and erecting poles to which the festoons would be attached.

The day before the bishop was due, it was perfectly clear that the triumphal avenue could not possibly be completed in time. Poles kept arriving, goodness knows from where, men kept digging holes, and our paper-lace factory became more and more frenetic. We ran out of paste, and Arcelia had to open a new sack of flour. We ran out of cord, and Arcelia had to wake up Chela to get some more. We worked late, still cutting and pasting. When we finally gave up and went to bed, not a single swag of paper lace had been draped from the church to the poles in the atrium or across the bishop's path from the airstrip to the gate.

I woke up early and dressed as quickly as I could in my enfeebled state. Although I didn't hurt nearly as much as I had at the start, I still had trouble getting my shoes on.

A Cora man was on the roof of the church when I limped out into the atrium. He was fastening the ends of long swags of paper lace to the little cross on top in the center of the facade. Three mestizos down below were grasping the other ends of the lacy, scalloped streamers as they floated down, to draw them out over the atrium and fasten them to the poles there. I counted the swags. There were twelve of them—green, blue, pink, and yellow—and they fluttered even though there seemed to be no breeze.

Fray Nicolas was leaning against the wall of the atrium, cutting pink tissue paper. He looked frantic. The poles were installed on both sides of The Street in Front of the Church, but they were bare. There was nobody in sight but Fray Nicolas and the men who were tying down the long, lacy festoons in the atrium.

I hobbled down the street. The poles turned the corner down by Mario's store, all of them bare. They filed out past the ramada to disappear down the hill I had struggled up the first time I had flown into

Jesús María. There was not one swag of paper lace in sight. It was obvious that the bishop's welcome was going to be a gigantic fiasco. I was as stricken as if the whole job had been my personal responsibility.

As I turned back toward the atrium, Don Gustavo came running toward me, his arms outstretched, paper lace on them piled up to his nose. Juana was running beside him, catching the strips that floated off the top of the pile. They ran past me without speaking. Juana gave me an agonized glance, cast her eyes to heaven, and ran on. I watched them as they disappeared down the hill.

While I was making my way back to the curato, two more men came running with paper lace draped over their outstretched arms, their wives running beside them. Arcelia came with her son Felipe. They all turned the corner on the far side of Mario's store.

The men who had been fastening the streamers to the poles in the atrium had finished. The old church had lacy swags in baby colors fanning out from the cross on the vaulted roof to the very wall of the atrium.

By the time the little plane buzzed three times over the town to announce its important arrival, by some incredible Mexican miracle, there were only three pairs of bare poles in The Street in Front of the Church and three streamers of paper lace to drape between them.

Almost everyone swarmed down to the airstrip, and I could imagine the scene down there. The bishop would alight from the plane, big, dark, modest, and benevolent as always. The mestiza women would crowd around him to kiss his ring. The Coras would shake his hand. Then, laughing and chattering, they would all escort him up the avenue that had got decorated just in time. Padre Domingo, meantime, would be hugging the children.

The crowd surged into the atrium with the bishop in the lead and the padre bringing up the rear, grinning with delight and carrying a little boy under each arm. I followed the crowd into the church.

The nuns had outdone themselves in preparing breakfast. We had it on long plank tables in the big, lofty room off the burros' entrance, where we had had the medicines before Madre Maria. There was tripe stew, with a hoof of the cow going into the bishop's bowl. There were mountains of tortillas brought in by the Coritas. There were eggs, and beans, and even a cake. Don Arnulfo came from the

Presidencia, and two new young teachers from Tepic, doing their year of social service. Don Serafim came from the Health Center, and a number of Coras, full of affection. When one shift finished eating, another shift sat down. It was a thoroughly joyous occasion.

As soon as I could climb into the Datsun, I headed for Guadalajara. I still hurt a lot, but, with a couple of aspirin every four hours, I managed pretty well. Getting into the plane seemed more awkward than before, the taxi ride in Tepic a little more hair raising, and the bus trip longer. I was glad to get home to a hot shower and a mattress.

Just as a precaution, I went to see the doctor who almost always sets our American bones. He ordered an x ray. I was in his office when he examined it. He looked at it closer and closer. Then he spoke.

"It's a miracle," he said. "A miracle."

He told me to sit still while he went to order crutches. When he came back, he brought two doctors with him to look at the x ray. My femur had been broken straight through, but the ends of the bone had stayed in place. They hadn't shifted a millimeter.

The doctors looked and looked. Then one of them whistled and turned to me, his eyes full of wonder.

"Señora," he said. "God loves you."

I wasn't really surprised. I had been suspecting it for quite a little while.

I waited until I was off my crutches before I went back to the Sierra.

21

Blessed All the Way

*I*t was the Day of the Dead.

I had just been blessed by Don Nazario, up in the Cora council house on the mesa of San Miguel. He had stood in front of the cluster of offerings spread out on the dirt floor. There were votive bowls made of gourds from the calabash tree, a few beautifully feathered arrows, some homemade candies. In one hand, he had a nosegay of the white perfumed flowers from trees that grow precariously on the sides of mountains higher up in the Sierra. In the other, he had a bowl, half a calabash shell, filled with water. He dipped the flowers in the water, sprinkled me in the form of a cross, and handed me the bowl. I drank. The water was sweet.

The only non–Indians in the dark, cavernous room were the bishop, Madre Maria, Madre Cristina, and I. We sat together on the heavy, rough-hewn wooden bench against the ancient brown stone wall. The tile roof peaked high above us, the rafters hung with the trappings of many fiestas: the long–nosed, blonde–haired mask of the buffoon of the Urraca dancers and the bullwhip he had threatened me with, now almost eight years ago; the wire cage to place on the lit–ter over Christ in the tomb, ready for its ribbons and flowers. The air was heavy with incense from the gum of the copal tree.

We watched as Don Nazario blessed the Coras who had been there before us. Then the bishop, large, kind, and majestic, stood in his brown Franciscan robe before Don Nazario, received his blessing, and took a sip of water from the gourd. Next, I was called up, then the madres. The Indians across the big dark room looked on with amused affection. They had given us a priceless vote of confidence. I was proud.

The fiesta had started the night before. Eight or nine young Coras, laughing and chattering, marched into the church during the Rosary. They headed straight for the alcove that had the coffin in it. Earlier in the afternoon, four laughing Cora youths had carried the coffin into the church on their shoulders. Now all the young men clustered around it.

The Rosary murmured on, with the faithful–all mestizos except me–praying our Hail Marys while the Indians opened the coffin, making audible jokes in Cora, laughing and pulling out shrouds.

The shrouds were yellowed, dirty, ragged. They looked as if they had been buried for a long, long time. Four of the youths put them on, tying the hoods under their chins, turning their backs to have their shrouds tied behind. Then, shrouded and unshrouded frolicked out of the church, the Muertos, or Dead Ones, making jokes and cooing in high falsetto like soprano doves. All through the night, the Muertos, with a growing band of laughing followers, trooped from house to house, begging food and drink and cooing in falsetto. The food was special–miniature tamales wrapped in tiny squares of corn husk, nickel-size cheeses, whole big squashes with ropes around their necks for carrying–and there was alcohol, always alcohol.

Lucio and Petra dispensed their offering from my Coca-Cola table, which we had lifted over to just inside my street door. Petra piled the cheeses and tamales on the table in a perfect pyramid, topping the pile with marigolds. Under the table she stashed the squashes and the potable alcohol that she and Lucio had bullied me into buying.

When the laughing chatter and high-pitched cooing signaled that the petitioners were upon us, Lucio and Petra went into instant action. Lucio ran out the door with plastic cups of alcohol. Petra ran out with handfuls of tamales and cheeses to pour into the woven baskets some of the men carried on their backs. Both of them ran out with the big crook-necked squashes. I knew they still mourned for Piedad, but they slipped out of the door with their flashlights to join the merry throng, laughing with the rest.

This morning in the council house there were mini-tamales and

micro–cheeses piled on a table in the corner of the room. After Don
Nazario had blessed us, three Coras surged off the floor, plunged their
hands into the pile, and came, grinning, to bring us handfuls of the
miniatures. The bishop, with admirable foresight, had brought a
small basket. The madres had the blue aprons of their brown habits. I
had only my bare hands, but the Coras filled them full.

With our thanks and the obligatory *"con permisos,"* "with your permission," we then slipped through the low, narrow door into the
November sun. There below us was spread out the whole town of
Jesús María. There was the massive old white church, towering above
the small, brown, tile–roofed houses, those of the mestizos decorously side by side along the cobbled street on the ledge upriver,
those of the Coras helter–skelter where the land widened out down-
stream. There beyond the town was the river, now a wide, blue, docile
brook. All around us were the mountains, every lovely shade of
green in the summer, now golded over, with only the tender green of
the occasional mesquite, the farther mountains brown with purple
shadows, the farthest of all a faint silhouette of faded blue. It was a
scene I had come to love.

As we picked our way down the lava flow, I could not help thinking how things had changed for me during the more than seven
years I had been living in Jesús María. I had come a stranger, the only
gringa among Cora Indians and mountain Mexicans, speaking little
Spanish and that badly, not even a Catholic in a town where religion
was at the heart of the lives of the Coras and the mestizos alike.

If Padre Domingo hadn't had all that medicine to classify, I would
have fled the first time the little plane buzzed back into the airstrip. If
I hadn't been the only person in town with medicine for dysentery
that first terrible August, I might not have lasted out a year. If I hadn't
been born lucky, Don Arnulfo might have run me out of town.

All that had happened more then seven years ago. What a long
time it seemed, as I slipped and slithered down the lava flow, the tiny
tamales and cheeses clutched in my two hands.

Don Arnulfo and his wife had become my friends. The Coras who
had sauntered into the Presidencia that day so long ago now made
themselves at home in the little clinic I shared with Madre Maria,
now that Padre Domingo had been transferred. Sometimes they came

for medicine or bandaging, but often just to see us, to sit and make jokes. Once in a while, one or another would slip a little present into my Cora bag: a few limes, a couple of eggs, a dried fish from the river. I now had nine godchildren, and their fathers and mothers, my "coparents," gave me the hand–to–shoulder salute every time we met, usually followed by a bear hug. They all tried to teach me to speak Cora and succeeded in borrowing money from me. I felt sure that Chela, my first friend, would be my friend for life and that Madre Maria would always be like a daughter to me.

It was true that I had never succeeded in working directly with a curandero. But then, after all, there was Goyo.

Goyo was a young Cora with double pneumonia. He had been sick for two weeks out in the mountains. At last, when he was almost dying, some of his friends improvised a stretcher with two sticks and a blanket and brought him down to Jesús María.

They installed him in an empty adobe house, hung blankets in front of his pallet to keep out the air, took offerings to the santitos in the church and the skulls in the cave, and cooked noxious concoctions over a little fire they had made between three stones on the dirt floor.

Pancho took me to see him. Pancho was a good friend. I had never found out his last name, or where he lived, or anything about him, really, except that he came to me when he was sick and quite frequently took me to see other victims who needed doctoring.

It was he who had taken me to see Jorge, when Jorge was so far gone he couldn't turn over, and all his relations were sitting on the floor with their backs against the wall, waiting for him to die. Pancho had shown me the medicine left by a government doctor who was passing through, medicine Jorge wasn't getting because there was no one in the family who could give shots. It was medicine for tuberculosis.

Pancho had kept watch as Jorge slowly regained his strength through the miracle of modern medicine and the milk and eggs I sometimes had to beg from the curato, as there were none for sale. In a couple of years, Jorge got well.

Jorge's relations had been grateful for my ministrations. The young Coras who surrounded Goyo were unanimously hostile. Pan–

cho insisted that they let me give poor Goyo medicine, but his friends hovered around me, breathing over my shoulder, demanding to know what medicine I was giving, and muttering among themselves.

We had a sterling young medical–school graduate in the Health Center then, one who would cheerfully enter a native house and risk fleas. He went to see Goyo with me and approved my treatment, only doubling the doses as the doctors so often did. The Cora companions had no more faith in him than they had in me and kept on muttering, but I persisted, fortified by the doctor's approbation and Pancho's unfailing support.

To take care of Goyo, I put off my monthly respite in Guadalajara. I got more and more tired, less and less forbearing. Finally, one afternoon as, hot and testy, I crouched through the door of the little adobe hut, I found a curandero there, bending over Goyo and sweeping the feathers of his arrows over Goyo's brow.

I forgot all about my desire to work with a curandero. After my struggle with Goyo's friends and in view of what, in my exhausted state, I was beginning to regard as a noble sacrifice of rest and a chance to speak English in Guadalajara, the presence of a shaman seemed like a personal affront. I had had enough.

"Well, well," I said. "So now we have a curandero. What good luck. Now I can go to Guadalajara."

The curandero turned around. It was Pancho.

"Cata! Cata!" he said. "Don't go. We need you. I'll be through here in a minute. Stick around!"

After a little sucking and spitting, he packed up his curing equipment and turned back to me.

"Didn't you know that I'm a curandero?" he asked me, incredulously.

"No," I said stupidly, remembering the times he had shanghaied me into going with him to visit somebody sick or hurt. He read my mind.

"How did you think I knew who needed you?" he asked me.

"But you came to me for medicine for yourself, too, Pancho."

"Of course," he said. "To you for medicine and to another curandero for curing. Don't go, Cata. We need you. We need both."

For many years had I not been thinking the same thing myself?

And although I had never found a curandero to work with, a curandero had, indeed, found me.

Goyo, of course, got well. How could he fail to with my kind of
medicine and Pancho's, too?

The bishop, the madres, and I reached the gravel strip in front of
my house. We smiled at one another, expressed the easy wish that all
would go well with each of us, and separated: the bishop and the
madres to go on down to the curato, I to show my booty to Chela.
There were three Coras on the steps of her store. They nodded with
amused affection to the bishop and the madres, and then they turned
to look at me. I knew them all. They had all come to me for medicine.
Sometimes they had demanded help for others. Could one of them
perhaps be a curandero? Could they all be curanderos? Would I ever
know? Did it really matter if I never knew?

They saw the cheeses and tamales in my hands, and all of them
grinned. I grinned back.

I ducked into my little house. I almost never bumped my head
anymore. Maybe, at last, I was beginning to learn to fit in.

Conclusion

Jesús María has changed since I first trudged up the hill from the airstrip on the flats. There is now a rutted road crossing the mountains all the way from Huejuquilla at the east end to Ruiz at the west. It cuts right through Jesús María, passing over the river at the Cora end of town on a splendid concrete bridge built by government engineers and dedicated by the president of Mexico himself.

A road is presumed to bring the blessings of civilization to an outpost as isolated as Jesús María. The blessings this road has brought are mixed.

The corn, which was once the economic tie between the Coras and the mestizos, has almost disappeared. There are few plantings now, and most of them are small. The big trucks that grumble in from outside bring quantities of packaged corn flour. By adding water to the dry powder, women can now make tasteless tortillas quickly in place of the delicious ones they used to make laboriously with freshly ground corn. The Coras, having no market for their harvest, can take their choice between starving a little and going to the coast to work for wages.

The side of the cliff that once glowed with sprays of rose-colored flowerlets now glitters with the silvery glint of empty tin cans.

Chela's kitchen no longer smells of torch pine fragrantly lighting the fire in the native stove. It now sometimes smells of gas from an unlighted pilot in the new four-burner.

In place of the whisper of burros pattering under sheaves of rustling corn, there is now the rumble of three-ton trucks and the grinding of gears. A bus clatters into town twice a week, a very uncomfortable bus with wooden seats.

Many houses are now restaurants for the burly truck drivers from Huejuquilla, Ruiz, and Fresnillo. Chela has one in my little house. It has a jukebox in it that blasts out American rock as soon as the generator revs up and the lights go on. She has solar energy for the bulbs that light up some of the compound when there is no juice from the town's generator. Luckily, it is not strong enough to run her new television.

There have been other changes.

The old church has been patched and painted. The new school is no longer new. The suspension footbridge still swings back and forth in the wind, but now it has huge gaps in its floor planks, revealing dizzying glimpses of the river below.

The new Presidencia proved so hot that the old Presidencia has been remodeled. With its thick old walls, it provides working space for the Presidente Municipal and his staff where they will not fry. With its new citified design, it adds a note of elegance to the old adobe town.

One can now buy fruits and vegetables in Jesús María.

Coras still pad down the aisle of the church with their white cotton disks and their purple nosegays, but most of them wear colorless, boughten shirts in place of those the women used to make by hand in gorgeous hues of bright magenta, hot orange, and sea green. In Holy Week, some of the boys run in rubber masks from Tepic in place of the handsome animal masks they used to make lovingly by hand.

Black-shrouded mestizas still visit the Virgin, but when government girls or tourist ladies come wearing pants, nobody but the bishop is scandalized.

The bishop is as kind as ever, but older. I am, too. I cannot climb into the back of a truck half as nimbly as I used to climb onto the back of a mule.

Some things never change. Jesús María is still a haven for scorpions, flies, mosquitoes, gnats, and other insects too uncivilized to mention. The hot, dirty wind still blows detritus into your eyes and grit into your teeth. After a rain, the earth still steams.

The heat worsted me in the end, just as it worsted the hearty nun from equatorial Africa. Still, I keep returning from time to time. For me, Jesús María is and always will be beautiful.

I strain for a view of it from the road down from El Cerro.

There it is, the noble old church towering over the little houses, some of them with their adobe now plastered over and painted white, like the church. There are the mountains sheering up behind, always changing and always beautiful. There is the river down below, studded with rocks in the dry season, a raging torrent in the rains.

And I know that when I clumsily climb down from the truck, I will receive the *abrazos*, the embraces, that tell that I am still not an outsider–that here in Jesús María, I will always be at home.

About the Author

*C*athcrine P. Finerty was born and raised in southern California but spent her professional life in Manhattan working as an advertising copywriter and a magazine editor.

After retiring, she moved to Mexico, eventually finding her way to the village of Jesús María in the Sierra Madre, where she lived for eight years and volunteered as a health care provider in a primitive clinic. This book comes out of her experiences there.

Catherine Finerty subsequently moved across the mountains to a smaller and more isolated Huichol community, where she continued her medical work until the Mexican government provided a doctor.

She now resides in Pomona, California.

"AN ADVENTURE, A WITNESS
TO AN EXOTIC AND NOW
DISAPPEARING CULTURE, AND
AN EXAMPLE OF WHAT A
RETIRED BUT STILL ENER-
GETIC AMERICAN CAN DO
WITH THE LATTER YEARS OF
LIFE." —BRUCE BERGER

*W*hat do most career women do after a
successful run on Madison Avenue?

Catherine Finerty watched her friends settle into the
country-club life. She opted instead for Mexico.

Soon after moving to Guadalajara, Finerty found herself
visiting small settlements hidden deep in Mexico's
tropical mountains. It was in Jesús María—so isolated
that one could get there only by mule or small plane—
that she found her new calling as the village nurse.

With its bugs and heat, no phones or running water,
Jesús María was hardly a place to enjoy one's retirement,
but Finerty was quickly charmed by its community of
Cora Indians and mestizos. *In a Village Far from Home*
richly describes this remote village with its festivals,
traditions, and a cast of memorable characters you'd
expect in a novel. Finerty's story takes readers deep into
the Sierra Madre to reveal its true treasure: the soul of a
people.

CATHERINE PALMER FINERTY was born and
raised in southern California and spent her professional
life in Manhattan working in advertising and magazine
editing. After spending eight years in Jesús María, she
continued her medical work in a smaller, more isolated
Huichol community. She now lives in Pomona, California.

THE UNIVERSITY OF ARIZONA PRESS
TUCSON, ARIZONA 85721
WWW.UAPRESS.ARIZONA.EDU

COVER PHOTOGRAPHS OF AUTHOR (FRONT) AND JESÚS MARÍA
(BACK) BY MICHAEL FINERTY. AUTHOR PHOTOGRAPH (BACK)
BY BRAD WITT.

ISBN 0-8165-2037-2

9 780816 520374